SALFORD

AN ILLUSTRATED HISTORY

SALFORD

AN ILLUSTRATED HISTORY

Glynis Cooper

breedon books
PUBLISHING

First published in Great Britain in 2005 by
The Breedon Books Publishing Company Limited
Breedon House, 3 The Parker Centre,
Derby, DE21 4SZ.

Dedication
For Hayley, a newcomer to Salford,
so that she will understand the city.

ISBN 1 85983 455 8

Printed and bound by CPI Group, Bath Press, Bath, Avon.

Salford's History

Introduction

The name Salford comes from the 'sallows' or willows that grew along the banks of the River Irwell (and some still remain in Lower Broughton near the City of Salford) and a crossing or ford across the Irwell. There was also Broughton's Ford across the Irwell at Pendleton and Woden's Ford near Hulme Hall on the Manchester borders.

The River Irwell in Salford as it looks today.

It requires quite a leap of the imagination to see Salford as it was maybe 5,000 years ago when the area was first actively settled by Neolithic farmers. It was well wooded and, in fact, Salford is described as still being forested by the time of the Domesday Book in 1086. The woodlands were deciduous and included oak, ash, elder, hazel and, close to water, willow (which likes a moist environment) could often be found growing. There was a ford across a low-lying part of the River Irwell at about the point occupied by Victoria Bridge today and close to where the lost River Dene tumbled into the Irwell. Willow trees grew along the banks of the Irwell here and summer flowers bloomed among the grasses. It was a quiet, pretty, rural spot with nothing much to disturb the peace, except birdsong and maybe the lowing of a few grazing cattle from the meadows of Piccadilly. Roe deer and wild boar inhabited the woods and came down to the river to drink from the clear waters. Sometimes a raised human voice could be heard, a childish shout of excitement carried on the wind or the deeper questioning voice of an adult working on one of the few small farming crofts that lay on the green triangle of land on the west bank of the river. A couple of sailing flats, small boats with a shallow draught, might be tied up at a makeshift landing stage. The river was teeming with fish, which offered a rich supply of food. Gradually, a small hamlet grew up on the green triangle of land, encouraged by the proximity to water, the fertile soil, the abundant fishing and the travellers who used the ford by the willows as a crossing point of the Irwell and brought their trade with them.

North-west towns and cities have altered beyond recognition over the last two centuries. There has been enormous urban, industrial and

A Mexican restaurant in Salford, an example of the massive regeneration that has taken place.

population growth; political boundaries have been redrawn; new metropolitan councils set up; redevelopment and regeneration, until the whole resembles an ever-changing kaleidoscope pattern. It is important, therefore, to define the various terms and places and to establish that this book is the history of Salford as it is today and not what used to be known as the Salford Hundred.

The area that was known as the Salford Hundred was much larger and older than the City of Salford and covered the City of Manchester but, confusingly, not all the places that now make up the City of Salford. The Salford Hundred was originally a mediaeval designation and in 1830 was listed as including: Bolton Parish (18 townships), Bury Parish (6 townships), Deane Parish (10 townships), Radclyffe Parish (1 township), Wigan Parish (1 township), Eccles Parish (5 townships), Flixton Parish (2 townships), Manchester Parish (30 townships which included Salford), Prestwich-cum-Oldham Parish (10 townships), Ashton-under-Lyne Parish (1 township), Middleton Parish (8 townships) and Rochdale Parish (8 townships).

Today most of those parishes come under Greater Manchester, and the City of Salford constitutes Salford plus a group of eight towns, which include: Eccles, Worsley (of which the district of Walkden is a part), Clifton, the twin towns of Pendlebury and Pendleton, Swinton, Irlam (including Chat Moss) and Cadishead.

Parliamentary Salford consists of 20 electoral wards: Barton, Blackfriars, Broughton, Cadishead, Claremont, Eccles, Irlam, Kersal, Langworthy, Little Hulton, Ordsall, Pendlebury, Pendleton, Swinton North, Swinton South, Walkden North, Walkden South, Weaste and Seedley, Winton and Worsley and Boothstown.

Salford Borough (as it was in 1904) '...lay within a great loop of the River Irwell...roughly three quarters of a mile from north to south and one mile from east to west...' In 1905 Salford township was described as: '...the shape ...of a boot with its toe to the north east and the sole along the south east...the toe piece joins a rough square within a bend of the Irwell, and the heel and ankle piece form a much larger square...the smaller square is the real Salford... the larger square is liberties ...Oldfield, Cross Lane and Ordsall...the western boundary of Salford began at Irwell near Mode Wheel, along a brook north of Regent Road towards Bolton Road turning to the Irwell at Lark Hill (now Peel Park), crossing the river and opposite peninsular in a curving line, the Crescent, formerly known as Broken Bank...and ran in a straight line to the south east corner of Broughton (on the Irwell); and... crossed Bolton Road to Pendleton border...'

The histories of Salford and its townships have been written as separate chapters because, unlike Manchester and its suburbs, Salford itself was only a village until the 19th century and the townships were independent and separate until the late 19th and 20th centuries. The City of Salford as it is today, and with which this history is concerned, has only existed since 1974. The first chapter on Salford is about the original Salford, and subsequent chapters tell the history of the other townships that make up the present city. There are also sections on items of individual interest, such as William Crabtree, the Salford astronomer who helped Jeremiah Horrocks to discover the Transit of Venus; Chat Moss, which was a wild, wet, lonely area of peat and moss until the 19th century and on which Irlam and Cadishead now stand; coal and canals; the legend of Ordsall Hall; strange stories and famous folk of Salford. In the chapter on Salford's history items of note have been outlined in a roughly chronological order to draw the reader's attention to important features and elements in the make-up of Salford's past and to give some idea of what life was like in each period of its history.

Although the City of Salford has suffered from unemployment, housing and social problems during the last 40 years, it is trying to address these problems now. There are regeneration schemes and new house building schemes and youth opportunities schemes; although it is a sad comment of the times that the modern Salford Opportunities Centre needs bars and shutters on the windows and doors because of the current culture of vandalism and violence that plagues parts of Salford. Nevertheless, the city appears determined that the next 40 years will see a reversal in fortunes and that, although Salford can never return to the pretty, peaceful little riverside village it once was, the way forward is to make the city a pleasant place in which to live once again and to capitalise on its educational resources and service industries for the future. The more urban townships of Pendlebury and Pendleton, Barton, Eccles and Swinton are looking to follow the city's example, while the outer, more rural, townships of Worsley, Cadishead and Irlam are closer to their goal and trading on their proximity to the fresh green countryside that Salford once was.

Acknowledgements

With grateful thanks to the staff of the Archives and Local History Studies Department at Manchester Central Library and to Tim Ashworth of Salford Local History Library.

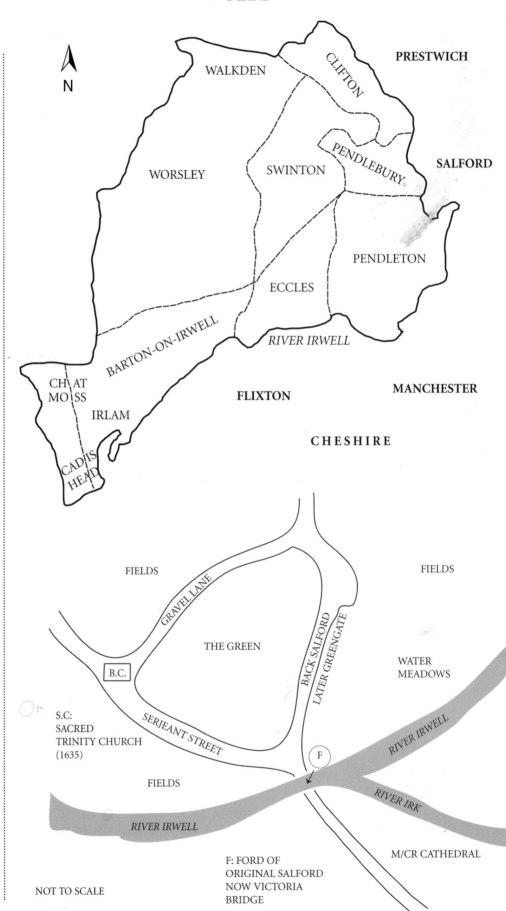

Sketch map of independent townships, which constitute the City of Salford since 1974.

DEANE

PRESTWICH

N

WALKDEN

CLIFTON

WORSLEY

SWINTON

PENDLEBURY

SALFORD

PENDLETON

ECCLES

RIVER IRWELL

BARTON-ON-IRWELL

CHAT MOSS

IRLAM

CADIS HEAD

FLIXTON

MANCHESTER

CHESHIRE

Sketch map of Tudor Salford

FIELDS

FIELDS

GRAVEL LANE

THE GREEN

BACK SALFORD LATER GREENGATE

WATER MEADOWS

B.C.

S.C: SACRED TRINITY CHURCH (1635)

SERJEANT STREET

F

RIVER IRWELL

FIELDS

RIVER IRK

RIVER IRWELL

M/CR CATHEDRAL

F: FORD OF ORIGINAL SALFORD NOW VICTORIA BRIDGE

NOT TO SCALE

Salford Timeline from the Domesday Book to 1939

Salford Cross in 1900. (Manchester Archives and Local Studies Library, Central Library)

1086   Roger de Poitou is recorded as holding Salford, in which there are '...three hides and twelve carucates of waste land a forest three leagues long and the same broad...there are many hays and a hawk's aery there...'

1142   Hamlet of 'Kereshall' is granted to Lenton priory so that '...a place could be built for the service of God...'

1169   'Sauford' is mentioned in Pipe roll.

1177   First mention of 'Ordeshalle'.

1182   Grant of Kersal to Lenton Priory confirmed by Henry II.

1199   King John gives Pendleton to Iorweth de Hulton in exchange for Broughton and Kersal woodlands.

1200   King John confirms the grant of Kersal village to Lenton Priory.

1220   Chantry chapel is founded at Pendleton.

1212   Gilbert Notton rented Cadishead from King John.

1226   First mention (in Lancashire Inquisitions) of a bridge over the River Irwell connecting Salford and Manchester. Salford is mentioned as 'Sainford'.

1228   On 4 June Henry III granted Salford a weekly market on Wednesdays and an annual fair on the 'eve, day and morrow of the Nativity of St Mary...' (7–9 September).

1230   Charter granted by the Earl of Chester making Salford a free borough.

1251   Ordsall granted to David Hulton by William de Ferrers, Earl of Derby.

1253   Assize Roll for Salford mentions de Selford and Shelford.

1257   Inquest on 'Saltford' (Salford).

1319   Hope granted by Earl of Lancaster to Sir Robert and Matilda de Holland.

1330   Ordsall passes to the Radclyffe family.

1351   Sir John Radclyffe claims Ordsall.

1353   Flemish weavers begin to settle in Ordsall village.

1368   First recorded mention of old Salford Bridge due to a bequest of £30 to the bridge from Thomas del Bothe, a yeoman of Barton upon Irwell, who had built a chapel on the bridge where prayers were said for the soul of the founder.

1373   First recorded mention of a maypole on Pendleton Green.

1399   Henry Bolingbroke, Duke of Lancaster and Lord of the Manor of Salford, becomes Henry IV, so Salford becomes a royal borough.

1450   St Katharine's Chapel built in Eccles.

1499   Erasmus stays at Ordsall Hall and is less than complimentary about it.

1505   Chapel on Salford Bridge is converted to a prison.

1526   Eruption of Chat Moss causes widespread disruption.

1539   After the Dissolution of the Monasteries, Pendleton is granted to the Bishop of Lichfield, Rowland Lee, and the Manor and Cell of Kersal are sold to Baldwin Willoughby.

1540   Andrew Barton of Smithills sells Salford Hall to Adam Byrom.

1570   First recorded mention of Weaste.

1574   Salford Hundred mustered 132 archers and 603 billmen under Sir Edmund Trafford and Sir John Radclyffe.

1575   Twenty-four 'croste grotes' (old coins) found in the grounds of a house belonging to George Bolton.

1588   Manchester flesh shambles (market) moves to Salford Bridge.

1590   Plague victims are buried in Hart Hill meadow at Buile Hill.

1604   Guy Fawkes is said to have originated the Gun Powder Plot at Ordsall Hall.

1605   Bad outbreak of the plague in Manchester and Salford.

1608   Jury of Salford found no cuckstool in the town and stated that unreasonable women might be put in the stocks or dungeon.

1610   William Crabtree born.

1639   Transit of Venus.

1634   Sacred Trinity Church founded by Humphrey Booth.

1666   Hearth Tax returns.

1745   Bonnie Prince Charlie passes through Salford on his way south.

1751   John Byrom writes the hymn *Christians Awake*! at Kersal Cell and sings it to his wife on Christmas morning.

1754   Pendleton Turnpike Trust turnpikes roads from Salford to Bolton.

1759   Work begins on the Duke of Bridgewater's canal from Worsley to Castlefield.

1765   Barton Aqueduct is built by James Brindley.

1777   Rival guisings between Eccles and Barton.

1786   First Sunday Schools opened in Salford.

1787   Building of New Bailey Prison begins.

1790   New Bailey Prison opens.

1796   Lying-in hospital is opened in the former Bath Inn in Stanley Street.

1797   Bury and Bolton Canal is virtually complete.

1798   Phillips and Lee Mill built.

1800   Bible Christian Church in King Street opened.

1805   Chat Moss drainage begun.

1806   Chapel Street becomes first street in the world to have gas lighting.

1809   Vegetarian Movement is founded by Revd William Cowherd.

1812   National Schools opened on Bolton Street and Great George Street.

1813   New Jerusalem Temple opens on Bolton Street.

1814   Cloth Hall on Chapel Street and Wesleyan Methodist Chapel on Brunswick Terrace both opened.

1816   Revd William Cowherd, founder of Bible Christian Sect and Vegetarian Movement, dies.

1817   Cadishead and Irlam 'civil war'.

1819   Independent Chapel on Chapel Street opened.

1819   James Joule born on Christmas Eve in New Bailey Street.

1820   Blackfriars Bridge opened.

1820   Gas Works opened.

1822   Swedenborgian conference, New Jerusalem Temple, Bolton Street.

1824   1 January, the first omnibus service ran from Market Street, Manchester to Pendleton.

1824   2 February, Deaf and Dumb School on Stanley Street opened.

1824   30 August, Town Hall foundations laid.

1824   21 September, St Philip's Church is consecrated.

1824   Salford Cross and stocks in Greengate demolished.

1826   Broughton Suspension Bridge opened.

1826   St Philip's Church built.

1827   Wesleyan Methodist Chapel opened.

1827   Salford and Pendleton Royal Dispensary opened.

1828   Bombay Street Infants School opened.

1830   Liverpool and Manchester railway opens and William Huskisson MP, fatally injured in an accident on the railway, died in Eccles Vicarage.

1830   Salford Royal Infirmary built.

1831   Broughton Suspension Bridge collapsed while 60 Rifle Corps were marching across. Six were badly hurt.

1831   St Thomas's Church, Pendleton, and Christ Church consecrated.

1832   Salford becomes a parliamentary borough after the Reform Act.

1832   15 December, Joseph Brotherton elected first MP for Salford.

1834 New police court at New Bailey opened.

1835 July, Adelphi Swimming Baths opened.

1835 25 August, teetotal society the Independent Order of Rechabites were formed.

1835 Salford Gas Works built on Lamb Lane.

1837 Victoria Mills, Weaste, built.

1837 12 July, cattle market opened on Cross Lane.

1838 29 May, Salford to Bolton railway opened.

1838 31 May, Broughton Zoological gardens opened.

1838 23 June, Salford Mechanics Institute opened.

1839 20 June, Victoria Bridge opened at cost of £20,000.

1839 Salford Lyceum held first meeting.

1839 St John the Evangelist in Higher Broughton consecrated.

1839 Manchester and Salford Junction Canal opened.

1839 George Bradshaw printed the first Bradshaw's Railway Timetable Guide in Barclay Place, Regent Road; the guide became very famous and is mentioned by Sherlock Holmes several times in Conan Doyle's books.

1840 James Joule establishes his laboratory at Pendlebury.

1842 St Matthias's Church is consecrated.

1842 St Bartholomew's Church is consecrated.

1842 St John's Church, Irlam, is consecrated.

1842 Higher Broughton Methodist Chapel opened.

1846 Swinton Industrial Schools open.

1848 Cathedral is completed.

1849 The country's first free public library opens in Salford.

1850 Charles Dickens visits Swinton Industrial Schools.

1850 Public Libraries Act passed.

1861 Cotton famine begins.

1865 Cotton famine ends but the damage is done.

1877 Eccles Wakes abolished.

1887 Last coal carried on the underground canal.

1889 Salford becomes a county borough.

1890 Cathedral is consecrated.

1894 Manchester Ship Canal and Salford Docks opened by Queen Victoria.

1905 No. 9 dock is opened by King Edward VII and Queen Alexandra.

1909 L.S. Lowry moves to Pendlebury and lives and paints there for 40 years.

1914 Top cotton exports from Salford Docks.

1915 Boots begin manufacturing in the Adelphi building.

1925 Cotton industry starts to decline.

1926   Salford is given city status.
1933   Walter Greenwood writes *Love on the Dole* during the
        Depression.
1937   Bull's Head on Greengate is destroyed by fire.
1939   Last working coal mine in Salford closes.

The timeline is by no means a complete chronological record. It merely highlights some of Salford's historical landmarks over the last nine centuries.

Salford's History

For so many centuries Salford was simply a small 'township' on the banks of the Irwell and scarcely worth the note of historians. It was, therefore, usually identified as Salford Hundred, which covers a large area, much more than the present City of Salford.

The New Lancashire Gazetteer or Topographical Directory 1830 describes Salford Hundred thus:

'*...Salford, a hundred bounded on the north by the hundred of Blackburn, on the west by the hundreds of Leyland and West Derby, on the south by the rivers Mersey and Tame, and on the east by Yorkshire. It contains five market towns, ten entire parishes, and a part of two others, comprising 102 townships, 78,537 houses, and 475,096 inhabitants. The hundred of Salford, after the metropolis, is the most thickly peopled district in the kingdom, though its soil is not generally fertile, and it contains several uncultivated moors and sterile morasses; coal, however, is abundant, and the plentiful supply of that important fossil has brought into existence workshops and factories in almost every township and supplied materials for human industry in every village. Canals, excavated in every direction, have also contributed to the universal intercourse; the country in general is flat, but on the Yorkshire side are some hills of considerable elevation, and the course of the rivers Irk and Irwell, north of Manchester, are distinguished by high and steep banks. At the original division of parishes in England, Salford was thinly peopled, which accounts for their small number in this now crowded district. Few of the great landed proprietors reside in their ancient halls and mansions, having sought a retreat in counties where land was less valuable, and rural enjoyment were less disturbed by the encroachments and bustle of manufacturing occupations...*'

Salford had begun life as a small settlement, which slowly grew up over the centuries around the crossing of the River Irwell, between Manchester and Salford, until the Industrial Revolution of the 18th century catapulted the village into a major centre of manufacturing and engineering and established it as one of the world's biggest dockyards, changing the face of the village forever. The village, which had no real history until the 18th century, mushroomed into a city within 50 years, with inventions, innovations and institutions seeming to spring up overnight. For clarity and simplicity, therefore, this book will detail the individual histories of Salford – the village that grew into a city – and the independent and very separate townships that eventually grew into the City of Salford and the metropolitan borough.

The Salford area seems to have been attractive to prehistoric societies. There is an excellent list of prehistoric remains given in the Manchester and Salford Exhibition Catalogue for Queens Park Art Gallery, which is reprinted in the Lancashire and Cheshire Antiquarian Society proceedings for 1909, vol. XXVII from the Neolithic (New Stone Age) period, there are flints and chips, flint knives and cores and a spindle whorl, which were found on Kersal Moor, a flint core discovered in the river gravel near Ordsall railway station and a flint knife found in the grounds of Irwell House, which stood near the river in Lower Broughton opposite the Lewis Recreation Ground.

Neolithic Salford would have been quite heavily wooded and full of deer, rabbits and wolves. It was during this period that previous hunter-gatherer tribes started to settle in small villages, felling some of the trees and farming the land. The 'slash and burn' method is thought to have been used; meaning that the trees were simply felled and burned, the wood being used as fuel for home fires. Some of the timber may have been used for building simple huts. The habitation sites were likely to have been close to the river for a ready water supply and the additional bonus of an abundance of fish, but the flint workings were usually on higher ground close to the source materials needed. Oats, a little barley, emmer and einkorn wheat crops would have been grown. Emmer and einkorn wheat varieties remained popular into Roman times and beyond. Research has shown that they offer a higher yield than modern wheat crops, and, because the glumes are stickier, they are less vulnerable to decimation of the crop by birds.

In the Bronze Age that followed, the settlements remained on the low fertile farming ground, but burials, particularly those of higher ranking villagers and chieftains, took place on higher ground, overlooking the lands that the dead person would have owned or lived on in life. The body, or an urn which contained the ashes of cremation, would be placed on the ground and an earthen mound would be built up over the top. Some of the mounds were quite large and visible from some distance. A Bronze Age cinerary urn containing 'calcined bones' was discovered beneath a small mound in the grounds of Old Broughton Hall (close to the Manchester boundary) in 1873. Though it began towards the end of the Neolithic period, it was in the Bronze Age that Britain became a 'ritual landscape' characterised by stone circles, henges, standing stones and cursii (parallel stone banks running sometimes for miles but always associated with one or more of the stone features mentioned). There would have been such features in the Salford area, but the sites would have been long since robbed for stone and subsequently covered by buildings during the last 200 years.

A number of Bronze Age finds were made during the excavation of the Manchester Ship Canal, demonstrating that the settlement sites had been close to the River Irwell. These include a stone hammer axe found near Mode Wheel in 1890; the Cadishead Celt (11ins x 3.75ins) found in the 1890s (which was a polished stone tool with flattened edges and may have had a ritual use) and a bronze looped spearhead from Irlam. Most interesting were two dug-out canoes that were discovered near Barton. One, a simple log dug-out, lay 400 yards away from the river, about 600 yards east of Barton Bridge. It measured 13ft 8ins long by 2ft 7ins fore and 2ft 2ins aft. The other, found in June 1890, was lying 25ft below the surface in the Trafford Hall cutting, just east of Barton Bridge. It was a '...hollowed, small trough, dug-out...' measuring 9ft 6ins long by 2ft 4ins width by 11ins deep. The '...bow does not project as in the larger example and it had a more curved stem...'

The Celts came to Britain during the Iron Age (probably around 500 BC), bringing their iron working skills with them. They were a fierce, artistic, vibrant and passionate people and many of their beliefs and traditions still survive today. A bride wearing white and carrying flowers to her wedding are customs that date back to Celtic times. The Celts worshipped a mother Goddess, believing the female to be the giver of life and, therefore, the symbol of fertility and continuance of the species (human, animal, plant, vegetable or crop). Their major festivals were based on the agricultural cycle: Imbolc – the Festival of the Lambs on 1 February; Beltane – the beginning of summer on 1 May; Lughnasadh – the harvest on 1 August; Samhain – old year's eve on 31 October (hence the tradition of the spirits of the dead walking, which were associated with the dying year) and new year's day on 1 November. Those were the old Celtic seasons and even today Beltane is a national holiday (although the customs of lighting bonfires and going a-maying [collecting greenery in the early morning] have largely lapsed) and Samhain is widely celebrated as Hallowe'en.

The Brigantes were the major Celtic tribe in the north of England, controlling much of the countryside. Their main stronghold in the Manchester/Salford area was the sandstone outcrop on which Manchester Cathedral stands, but they would have farmed and grazed their cattle on the fertile lowland across the river and may, in fact, have encouraged settlement there to establish ownership of the western side of the river crossing. The Brigantes were certainly the major factor in Agricola's decision in AD 79 to build a large Roman fort at Castlefield in Manchester (not far from the present Salford borders) to protect the main routes to York, Chester and Carlisle and the salt ways across the Pennines from the Cheshire wiches. This powerful Celtic tribe knew the territory well and adopted guerilla warfare tactics, which the highly trained

Roman military machine was not equipped to deal with. Try as they might, the Romans never succeeded in crushing the Brigantes, despite the betrayal of their Queen, Cartimandua, who collaborated with the Romans so that they would rid her of the husband she hated and leave her free to marry Venutius, the Roman overlord of York, with whom she had fallen in love.

Salford lay near the Roman fort at Castlefield and a Roman road to Coccium, better known today as Wigan, (following approximately the line of the present Regent Road, which was called Back Lane on Green's map of 1793) divided '...the larger square...Oldfield, Cross Lane and Ordsall...in half so that Ordsall lay on the south-west side...and passed through Worsley'. In the vicinity of Boothstown Quarry around 540 Roman coins, hidden in two pots, were dug up close to a former cotton mill at The Delph in 1947. The coins were dated from AD 251–275. Another hoard of third-century coins, this time between 800–1,000, were discovered in 1989 during the construction of a new housing estate at Booth's Bank (close to Worsley). A Roman centurion's ring was found on the site of St John's Church Institute at Pendlebury in 1912 and some Roman coins in the adjacent rectory grounds.

The route of the Manchester–Wigan road on the OS map of 1849 was detailed in the notes of the Revd Edmund Simpson from Ashton-in-Makerfield. He traced the road from what would have been the west gate of Manchester, crossing the Irwell at Woden Ford at Ordsall (close to the haunted Hulme Hall), then running along the line of Regent Road in Salford and Hodge Lane, across Pendleton Fields and through Eccles, past Hope Hall and Chorlton Fold (between Monton and Swinton) and close to Drywood Hall in Worsley. The road was discovered near Worsley when the Eccles–Wigan railway line was built. It lay about a foot below ground level and appeared to be about 21ft wide. In 1957 parts of this road were excavated just north of Worsley, less than six inches below the ground surface. Here it was 13ft wide with the typical Roman drainage ditches each side. Similar drainage ditches can be seen running along the side of modern Spanish roads. The road appeared to have been built using locally quarried stone from The Delph. A second Roman road ran along what is now the A6, passing through Walden and Little Hulton, and there are traces of a crossing at Pendleton Brook by the Roman road to Ribchester, which followed the route of Bury New Road. Although the Romans finally left Britain in AD 410 at the end of 'the long sunset', their roads continued to be used for centuries afterwards by both the indigenous Celts and by new peoples who arrived to claim and reshape the land.

The Angles and Saxons arrived a few decades after the Romans had left. They were savage fighters and understood, better than the Romans, the Celtic *modus operandi*, and it was they who defeated and dispossessed the Celtic tribes in a way that the Romans had never quite managed to do. It was the Saxons who laid down the settlement pattern of the countryside, which is still discernible today. In Anglo-Saxon times, boundaries were often marked with crosses and a Saxon cross shaft was discovered near Eccles Church during the Manchester Ship Canal excavations. Later, some of these crosses were moved to the centre of the town or village, where they served as a focal point for markets, public announcements, punishment of miscreants and the general social life of the town. An early mediaeval cross was found at Barton Old Hall. Often, however, the existence of a cross is remembered only in place name evidence like Cross Lane.

There is no record of Danish occupation of Salford. Possibly it was too small to be of much interest to them or to offer much resistance. Manchester was so badly damaged by the Danish invaders that it has been suggested that it was of little interest to William the Conqueror and that it was why the Salford Hundred (Salford itself being too small to be of note) was the main unit of the area recorded in the Domesday Book. By 1066 the Salford Hundred (or Manor), also known as the Salford 'wapentake' or Salfordshire, belonged to King Edward the Confessor. At this time the land was mostly forested and divided into 21 'berewicks', or sub-manors, for legal and taxation purposes. There was also a 'Hundred Court', which dealt with small claims and public matters. Unusually, the Salford Hundred Court survived into the 19th century.

After the Norman Conquest of 1066, the lands were taken from their Saxon owners and distributed among the followers of William the Conqueror as rewards and thanks for fighting services rendered. In the Domesday Book, the Norman inventory of English (or former Anglo-Saxon) settlements and possessions taken in 1086, Roger de Poitou was recorded as owning the Manor or Hundred of Salford. Several places in the Salford area are mentioned in the Domesday Book and a number of simple canoes dating from this period have been recovered from the Irwell and the Mersey. They were used for transporting turf, peat, people and goods.

Although there was ecclesiastical and some commercial activity in Manchester during the 1100s, nothing much is known of Salford in this period, although it is fairly certain that Salford shared the agricultural activities and same cottage textile industries of wool and linen as its larger neighbour across the Irwell. In 1230 the Earl of Chester granted a Charter to Salford making it a free borough, which laid the foundations of local government for over 500 years. His seal showed a feudal knight. Salford's armorial bearings, granted in 1844, have three gold wheat sheaves on a blue background as per the Earldom of Chester and thus provide a link to Norman and mediaeval times. However, despite the granting of the Charter, Salford was not recognized as a borough in the Municipal Corporations Act of 1833. After the granting of the Charter, Salford had its own 'Reeve' (a mediaeval administrator and keeper of law and order) and law court called the 'Laghemof', and this system provided the basis of local government until the police commissioners of 1791 were appointed.

Salford in 1650

The first known map of Salford dates from 1650. Small black and white timber-framed buildings are shown standing on Serjeant Street (which is now the road leading over Blackfriars Bridge to Chapel Street). The last of these timbered buildings was the Bull's Head on Greengate, which closed in 1931. The Tudor town had '...cottages with thatched roofs and daub walls, street 'mydinges', blocked water courses and primitive roads...'

Salford Bridge (which preceded the present Victoria Bridge opposite the Cathedral) lay on the site of the old ford, which had been the only link with Manchester. Houses clustered around the triangular market place with its nearby stocks and court house. The Court Leet met here and the Portmote records are preserved in Salford Museum.

The triangular plan and layout was still basically unchanged in 1740. The more modern town initially focused around Sacred Trinity Church, built in 1634 on Chapel Street and known as the Flat Iron Church.

Wesley Chapel, Irwell Street, in 1830. (Manchester Archives and Local Studies Library, Central Library)

Salford at war

Salford suffered some troubled times during the 17th and 18th centuries as, while Manchester was Parliamentarian during the Civil War (1640-1649), Salford was very much Royalist, and the siege of Manchester was launched from Salford at what is now Victoria Bridge. This was then the only crossing point of the Irwell between Manchester and Salford. The siege was soon over but did little to improve relations between the two towns.

A century later Salford proved itself staunchly Jacobite when Bonnie Prince Charlie marched into the town in 1745. Before leaving to take London by storm, he was blessed by the Revd John Clayton and he left Salford in high spirits. Bonnie Prince Charlie got as far as Derby before his generals decided that the risk was too great. Just nine days after leaving, the would-be king was back in Salford and forced to admit defeat. Two local men, Tom Syddall and Tom Deacon, who had joined the Manchester contingent to fight for the Jacobite cause, were captured and beheaded, and their heads were returned to Manchester where they were displayed on the Manchester Exchange.

Methodist Chapel, Irwell Street, in 1830. (Manchester Archives and Local Studies Library, Central Library)

Salford in 1750

In 1750 Salford was still quite small. The general shape of the town was a small triangle with its apex opposite the Cathedral and bounded by Salford Street (now Chapel Street), Back Salford (now Greengate), and Gravel Lane. Near the corner of Green Lane stood Salford Workhouse, where Samuel Bamford's father was the master for a time. Bamford was a Manchester mill worker who was one of the speakers at Peterloo in 1819 and wrote radical working class material and poetry. Behind the

Irwell Street Chapel in 1900. (Manchester Archives and Local Studies Library, Central Library)

workhouse stood the house of James Raffald (the husband of Elizabeth Raffald, who wrote a cookery book that is still in use and compiled a directory of Manchester and Salford). He was a gardener by trade and his nursery gardens extended to Gravel Lane. Opposite the Workhouse, Sandywell Lane led to the ford across the river in the direction of Broughton. On the corner of Sandywell Lane stood the Springfield estate, which, from 1819–26, would be the home of James Leech, a dyer who became the first person to grow marrows in England. A cockpit stood close to Sandywell Lane, which was eventually renamed Springfield Lane.

White Cross was part of Chapel Street and this area was known as Top Salford. The Portmote Records show wide strips of waste land lining the roadway here, on which 'the local burgesses allowed their pigs to roam…'

The Pearl Spring and its approach lanes were noted and so was Sandywell Lane. It was the end of an era and marked the end of rural Salford but no one knew this at the time.

Salford in 1821
In 1821 there were houses in Chapel Street as far as St Stephen's Street but only a few from there to The Crescent. Ackers Square in the Adelphi was in the midst of fields. Across the river, on higher land, was Lark Hill, which is now Peel Park. A field path led from The Crescent to Regent Road, and, crossing a bridge to Manchester, Hulme Hall lay not far away from the fields behind. Aston wrote a description of The Crescent in 1821.

'...in the other situation is the Salford Crescent which stands upon a spot almost unrivalled for a beautiful and commanding prospect, which, from the nature of the situation, can never be interrupted by buildings. The inhabitants of this charming elevation will always be sure of rich rural scenery in view of their front windows... the fertile valley, the meanderings of the river Irwell, approaching to and receding from the Crescent, the rural cots, the pleasant villa, the rising hills and the distant mountains...'

Salford Bridge and oratory in 1860. (Manchester Archives and Local Studies Library, Central Library)

A three-storey Victorian House, c.1950. (Manchester Archives and Local Studies Library, Central Library)

Unfortunately, Mr Aston reckoned this before the invention of the internal combustion engine, but he had no way of knowing that in 1821, since the advent of the first motor car still lay 75 years into the future. The Crescent was widened in September 1963 and today a very fast road, constantly buzzing with four lanes of traffic, separates The Crescent from the River Irwell, which is mostly hidden from view by overhanging trees; but in comparison with much of Salford, The Crescent is not a bad place to live. During the 1930s *Hobson's Choice* was filmed on the banks of the Irwell by The Crescent and then moving along near Salford Royal Hospital, St Philip's Church and the Cathedral.

The River Irwell from The Crescent as it looked in 1830, before the invention of the motor car. (Manchester Archives and Local Studies Library, Central Library)

A photograph of The Crescent today, a busy road in Salford.

Salford in 1911

From 'SALFORD.' *LoveToKnow 1911 Online Encyclopedia.*

©2003, 2004 LoveToKnow.

http://48.1911encyclopedia.org/S/SA/SALFORD.htm

SALFORD, a municipal, county – and parliamentary borough of Lancashire, England, 189 m. N.W. by N. of London and 31 m. E. by N. of Liverpool. Pop. (1908 estimate), 239,234. Salford also gives its name to the hundred of south-west Lancashire in which Manchester is situated...the parliamentary and municipal boundaries of Salford are identical; area, 5170 acres. The parliamentary borough has three divisions, each returning a member. The borough, composed of three townships identical with the ancient manors of Salford, Pendleton and Broughton, is for the most part separated from Manchester by the river Irwell...at the other extremity of Salford it joins the borough of Eccles. The chief railway station is Exchange station, which is in Salford, but has its main approach in Manchester. The Lancashire & Yorkshire and the London & North-Western railways serve the town...

In 1634 Sacred Trinity Church (Salford Chapel) was built and endowed under the will of Humphrey Booth the elder, who also founded charities which have grown greatly in value. The yearly income of more than 17,000 is disposed of in pensions and in hospital grants. His grandson, Humphrey Booth the younger, left money for the repair of the church and the residue is distributed amongst the poor. The yearly revenue is about £1400. Salford is the seat of a Roman Catholic bishopric, and its cathedral, St John's, with its spire of 240ft., is the most noteworthy ecclesiastical building in the borough....the chief public buildings are the museum and art gallery at Peel Park, the technical school, the education offices and the Salford Hospital. The town hall, built in 1825, is no longer adequate for municipal needs. Broughton and Pendleton have each a separate town hall. The large and flourishing technical school was developed from a mechanics institution.

Peel Park, bought by public subscription in 1846, was the first public recreation ground in the borough. In the grounds are Langworthy Gallery and a museum. In the park are statues of Queen Victoria, the Prince Consort, Sir Robert Peel, Joseph Brotherton and Richard Cobden. The only other monuments are South African War memorials...almost opposite Peel Park. Other

parks are at Seedley, Albert and Buile Hill; the last contains a museum, the contents of which have been transferred from Peel Park. There is also Kersal Moor, 21 acres of Moorland, crossed by a Roman road, which has been noticed for the variety of its flora, and for the capture of the Qecophara Woodielia, of which there is no other recorded habitat. The David Lewis recreation ground at Pendleton may also be named. Altogether Salford has thirty parks and open spaces having a total area of 217 acres. The corporation have also provided two cemeteries.

When the municipal museum was founded in 1849 a reference library formed part of the institution, and from this has developed a free library system in which there are also nine lending libraries.

The commercial and industrial history of Salford is closely bound up with that of Manchester. It is the seat of extensive cotton, iron, chemical and allied industries. It owes its development to the steam-engine and the factory system, and in recent years has shared in the increase of trade owing to the construction of the Manchester Ship Canal, which has added greatly to its prosperity. This will be seen by an examination of the rateable value of the three townships now comprised in the borough. This in 1692 was 1404; in 1841, 244,853; in 1884, 734,220; in 1901, 967,727; in 1908-1909, 1,022,172.

The municipal government is in the hands of a town council consisting of 16 aldermen and 48 councillors elected in 16 wards. The water-supply is from Manchester. The corporation have an excellent tramway service. There are also municipal baths. Salford has a separate commission of the peace.

There are no certain figures as to the population before 1773, when at the instance of Dr Thomas Percival a census was taken of Manchester and Salford. The latter had then 4755 inhabitants.

Census returns show that its population in 1801 was 14,477; in 1851, 63,850; and in 1901, 220,956. The death-rate in 1906 was 18.5 per thousand.

Heald's greengrocers, Dorset Street, Salford, c.1925. (Salford Local Studies Library)

Salford Town

Salford was classed as being in Lancashire but it lay in Manchester ecclesiastical parish and in Salford Poor Law Union. In 1792 the appointed police commissioners began to administer the township; but in 1844 Salford Borough was established, consisting of Salford township and part of Broughton township, and the borough authorities replaced the commissioners. Pendleton, the rest of Broughton and a part of Pendlebury were added to the borough in 1853, and in 1889 it became a county borough. In 1926 the borough was made a city, its motto being 'integrity and industry'. After the addition of a part of Eccles Borough in 1961, the city became a part of the much wider Salford Metropolitan District and received the official title of City of Salford in 1974. The new metropolitan district or 'city' embraced the City of Salford, which had been the former county borough; Eccles Municipal Borough; Swinton and Pendlebury Municipal Borough; plus Irlam and Worsley Urban Districts.

The City of Salford Coat of Arms

There are three gold wheat sheaves on a blue background from the arms of the Earl of Chester, who granted Salford its Charter in 1230. Also included are flying bees, which represent industry; a gold shuttle denoting the importance of the textile industry and chains, which are commemorative of engineering for which Salford was also renowned. The supporting wolf comes from the shield of the Earldom of Chester and the supporting antelope was the badge of King Henry IV, who was Duke of Lancaster. The whole coat of arms stands on a representation of grass in which grow the red roses of Lancaster, and the shield is topped by a 'white half-lion holding a lance with a blue flag and a gold shuttle'.

Industry in Salford

Domestic Industries before the Millscapes

Before the Industrial Revolution the Portmote records show that local cottage industries included cloggers and cobblers (there is a reconstruction of a clogging and cobbling workshop in Lark Hill Museum); spinning and weaving in cottages on Greengate and Chapel Street; whistlers or bleachers and dyers, for which Pendleton was the main centre, but there were also dye houses on the Salford side of the Irwell near Greengate, and brewing at the King Arms brew house behind the tavern of that name on Oldfield Road.

There was a Cloth Hall on Greengate for woollens and linens, before cottons, which was replaced in 1814.

Industries in the Industrial Revolution

The major industry, of course, was textiles, and other industries, while not actually textiles, were textile related. The river at Ordsall was lined with factories like Haworth's Spinning Mill (which had 4,000 employees), and vegetable dyes manufactured at Ordsall were used by calico printers. There were the Adelphi Bleachers and Dyers; Varley's Chemical and Bleaching Works on Whit Lane in the 19th century and the Pendleton Alum Works of Spence and Dixon in around 1850.

In 1850 there were 10 brass and iron founders in Salford and there were three in Pendleton during the latter half of the 19th century. Cast-iron bollards, lamp posts and railings were produced as well as mill fitments. Foundries included Bateman and Sherratt – iron founders from before 1800, who built the iron-framed mill of Phillips and Lee on Chapel Street – and Hodgkinsons's Mechanical Stokers, close to Pendleton Church, who had their own foundry near Liverpool Street.

A number of iron founders turned to engineering and became millwrights. Among these were the famous firm of Mather and Platt, who grew from a Salford foundry in Brown Street. Others included William Higgins (who was a cotton mill owner as well), who had a millwright's shop off Gravel Lane; George Wilson and Co., who had two works on Springfield Lane that lasted the length of the cotton boom; Hulse and Co Engineers; Smith and Coventry Cresley Iron Works; Lancaster and Tonge, Engineers; Farmer Norton on Adelphi Street, who made heaters and dryers for the textile industry (which closed in the 1980s and the factory was demolished) and Joseph Robinson of Pendleton.

There were also chemical industries. Hervey, Peak and Hervey on Ordsall Lane and Thoms, forerunners of Cussons and Colgate-Palmolive,

*Mather and Platt,
Salford Iron
Works. Steam
Engines,
Florence and
Grace, supplying
power to
overhead
shafting, c.1885.
(Salford Local
Studies Library)*

*Ordsall Lane,
which was the
site of a former
chemical works.*

were starch and soap makers. Boots (1915-1940) pharmaceutical works stood on Adelphi Street. They were succeeded by Kruschers Salts from Pendleton and then by Aspro. The building, now known as the Adelphi Building of the University of Salford, houses the University's Performing Arts and Media Studies Department. Chemical firms using coal tar and petroleum raw materials, like Lancashire Tar Distillers from Weaste, stood by the Manchester Ship Canal.

Brewing continued but on a rather more mass-produced scale. A tax and malt monopoly by the Irk Mills in Manchester resulted in breweries being set up in the surrounding townships. Many small such businesses stood near the Irwell. Following rationalization and reduction in around 1900, and using good water from deep sandstone borings, there were then six breweries. These were Groves and Whitnall (moved to Warrington in 1972); Walker and Homfroys; Threlfalls in Eccles; Townsend's Soft Drinks at Paradise Works on Greengate; Mottram's Brewery and the Cook Street Brewery of Whitbread.

Chapel Street Cornbrook Brewers, c.1948. (Manchester Archives and Local Studies Library, Central Library)

Cotton in Salford

The 19th century changed the face of Salford as it did many other towns. Until that point Salford had been little more than a village in pretty rural surroundings. Within a few decades it was transformed into a mill town full of cotton manufactories and engineering works, blackened forbidding buildings, smoking chimneys and row upon row of dark cramped little cottages overshadowed by the industry around them. This was the

Salford that Ewan MacColl sang about in *Dirty Old Town* and the Salford that L.S. Lowry portrayed so evocatively in his paintings. Cotton manufacture brought prosperity to a few but a miserable life to many. Child labour, working hours and conditions in the mills, the overheating of the spinning sheds and the underheating of the weaving sheds, lack of basic sanitation facilities and any real quality of life led to despair, disease and usually an early death. There are those who still dispute this, but the source materials are all there: the medical officer's reports, eye-witness accounts and official statistics make depressing and shameful reading.

It wasn't just the countryside that was lost but a whole way of life. The cows had never particularly minded if they were milked at 5.30am, 6.00am or 6.30am, just as long as they got milked. The same went for feeding pigs and hens, or grazing the sheep, but suddenly the working population of the new northern mill towns was thrown into a situation where if they were one minute late for work the factory gates had slammed shut and they lost a whole day's pay. They were forced to work long and rigidly set hours. Dinner was no longer taken in the fields, if it was taken at all, since the foremen, determined to get the most profit out of their workers, often found reasons for people to continue working through the dinner hour, which began and ended with a ringing bell or a siren. Fourteen-hour working days were considered normal, and in winter many workers never saw daylight. Taking an unauthorised break for any reason was seen as slacking and was a dismissable offence. The whole ethos was the most tremendous psychic shock and it scarred the quality of life. Today the mills have long gone but the mentality and the British obsession with the clock remain, a fact which bewilders our European counterparts, who escaped the excesses of the Industrial Revolution.

Mills lined the banks of the Irwell and the canals, their tall chimneys belching smoke that almost blotted out the sun. Most days it was as though the city lay in a thick fog. Agricultural labouring could be hard and harsh work, but it was much healthier than inside the mills where the air was choked with cotton dust, the spinning sheds could reach 80 degrees and the weaving sheds were freezing. Above all, there was the deafening incessant noise. Quarry Bank Mill in Cheshire and Queen Street Mill in Burnley are still working mills, running for the benefit of heritage and education. Visitors are advised not to remain in the spinning and weaving sheds for more than 15 minutes on account of the noise made by the machinery and the possible resultant damage to hearing – 15 minutes set against 14 hours a day six days a week 52 weeks a year for a lifetime. Most mill workers suffered some form of deafness and developed their own sign language since it was totally impossible to even yell across a weaving shed.

If it was bad for adults, it was worse for the children. From as young as seven they were expected to work a 12-hour day six days a week. It was wryly noted during the north-west's support for Abraham Lincoln's anti-slavery stance in the American Civil War (1861–5) that American slave children worked shorter hours in better conditions than English child workers. If the mill children slowed down or fell asleep on the job they were often savagely beaten. Children were smaller and more nimble than adults and so they were useful for cleaning underneath moving machinery without it requiring to be stopped, which would cost money. Accidents were common with cuts, bruising and loss of fingers the most usual injuries. For girls skirts were an added hazard. These would catch in unguarded machinery and some girls suffered horrific leg injuries. Two thirds of the workers in most mills were women and girls since they were cheaper labour.

As the factory system grew, the population soared from 12,000 in 1812 to more than 70,000 in 1840 and to almost a quarter of a million by 1900. In a little under 90 years the population had multiplied to 19 times its original size and the resultant overcrowding in squalid housing led to severe social problems. Statistics suggest that as many as 80 houses would be built on an acre of land. These took the form of one-up-one-down and slightly larger two-up-two-down terraced houses in endless rows and streets, mostly badly built by 'cowboys' (to use modern terminology) before the new building regulations of the 1840s came into force, back-to-backs (in which houses shared a common back wall so that there was no rear entrance or gaps between the houses) and the infamous courts. Salford suffered less from these courts, that had so horrified Friedrich Engels, than Manchester in that Salford had fewer of them. Workers cottages with basements would be built tightly packed around a court with central sanitation facilities. In practice this meant that as many as 300 people would have to share a single outdoor toilet. Whole families lived in single rooms in the basements of these dwellings, which were often flooded with untreated effluent. Diseases such as typhoid, typhus and tuberculosis were rife, to the despair of local medical officers of health. The only escape lay in drink and pubs, and gin palaces flourished. Drunkenness and its often attendant violence were common. Chapel Street and its surrounds was one of the worst slum areas.

Chapel Street by Flat Iron Market, c.1904. (Manchester Archives and Local Studies Library, Central Library)

Trade continued to expand, however, and the opening of the Salford Docks in 1894 on the newly built Manchester Ship Canal meant that Salford became '...an industrial meeting point for all major routes... receiving raw materials... [and] the main distribution point for manufactured goods being exported...' Many mills, such as those of Elkin Arbitrage, stood along the Bolton and Bury Canal in Pendleton; the Salford end of the canal being taken up with extensive coal yards. There was the Islington Twist Company cotton mill and close by lay the Gough, Slater, Smith and Rawson, Brotherton, and Higgins cotton mills, to name but a few, and by 1830 Walker's Silk Mill stood close to the coal yards. In 1905 the Acme Spinning Company built their first mill in Pendlebury,

*Midland Bank on
Chapel Street,
c.1960.
(Manchester
Archives and
Local Studies
Library, Central
Library)*

*Domed building,
Chapel Street,
c.1963.
(Manchester
Archives and
Local Studies
Library, Central
Library)*

which was the first electrically-driven cotton mill in the country, supplied with electricity by the Lancashire Electric Power Company. Two years later Acme purchased the Pendlebury Spinning Company Ltd mill (founded and built by James and Robert Knowles in 1855). At the time one mill owner remarked 'such a commercial edifice will stand the test of time'. Less than 20 years later cotton was in decline.

The cotton manufacturing industry of north-west England never really recovered from the cotton famine years caused by the American Civil War (1861–5). Nevertheless, there were highs and lows for the next half a century, culminating in unprecedented levels of trade exports in 1914 on the eve of World War One. This proved to be a swan song. China, India and Japan had been buying quantities of cotton manufacturing machinery and spun yarn for several years, and the manufacturers, blinded by the thought of quick profits, had not the foresight to realise what this might mean. In the aftermath of the Great War (1914–18) they found out. Instead of providing a ready market for buying cotton goods, China, India and Japan had begun to manufacture their own cotton goods and were selling them to their own people and back to Western countries, undercutting prices charged by British manufacturers. Then in 1925 Japanese cotton manufactories began 24-hour working, and the British cotton industry went into decline. During World War Two, as the bombs rained around them, all the British cotton manufacturers were concerned about was keeping the price of cotton up. It was a fatal mistake, and by the 1960s the British cotton industry was dead.

Irish Cellar Dwellers in Salford

In the mid-19th century Manchester was forced to cope with the scandal of 'Little Ireland': a wet and dingy low lying area by the River Medlock in Chorlton, which had become infamous for the deprived and appallingly filthy conditions in which many Irish labourers lived. Engels thundered his disapproval in his 1844 publication *The Condition of the Working Class in England*. The problem was that the neglect of Irish estates by absentee landlords and the Irish potato famine of the 1840s had resulted in thousands of deaths from hunger and despair and poverty for hundreds of thousands more Irish people. Desperate to escape in search of jobs and food, Irish immigrants poured into Manchester and Liverpool, lured by tales of what could be earned in the mills or on the railways. The reality was very different. Most people despised the Irish and they were often given the dirtiest and lowest paid jobs if they were given jobs at all. Many were forced to scavenge for food and to find shelter as best they could.

Because the Irish were poorly paid, when they were paid at all, they lived in the cheapest accommodation, which was often in the cellar of someone's house. Determined to squeeze as much as possible into as little as possible, those who mass-built the endless rows of back-to-backs, one-up one-down, two-up two-down and the infamous courts for workers in the mills and manufactories included cellars, which were at best damp and unhygienic. Medical Officers of Health and social reformers condemned the squalidness of these cellar dwellings and the potential they offered for bacteria to spread. Official consciousness was finally stirred into action by the realisation that when there was an outbreak of cholera or typhoid the disease refused to recognise class barriers and the wealthy merchants and mill owners and their families could be at just as much risk as the labourer in his hovel.

Salford had an Irish born population of 8.2 percent of the total, and in the light of Engels's accusation that most cellar dwellers were Irish and that they had a higher level of unemployment and lower standards of living and general health the Irish situation was carefully considered. Irish immigration, an 'urban phenomenon' of the time, had peaked between 1845–51. The Irish, it transpired, were variously employed in mills, gas works, paper making, sawyers, and as porters, coal carriers and navvies. Unemployment among the Salford Irish was not noticeably higher, but fewer Irish women went out to work and it was felt that the Irish situation in Salford was generally stable.

During the 1980s a survey of the Irish was carried out by M.W. Garret, using the census returns of 1861 and 1871, looking at the general view of the Irish and whether they tended to live in ghettos and form the majority of cellar dwellers. Eighteen percent of cellar dwellers in 1861 were Irish, but this had dropped to 15 percent by 1871. Therefore, it appears that Irish cellar dwellers were actually in a minority, and, although there '...was a pattern of clustering within the older parts...' such as Park Street or Ashton Street, Garden Street and Brown Street, '...nowhere within Salford was there a collection of streets in which Irish-headed households exceeded 50 percent of the population...' It was also obvious, from the figures given for cellar dwellers in the census returns, that the reduction in such clustering, as had occurred, was due to integration.

Year	non-Irish	mixed	Irish
1861	50%	37%	13%
1871	37%	57%	7%

(Garrett, M.W. *The Irish Community in England*, MMU, 1986)

Salford Independent Volunteers in 1805. (Manchester Archives and Local Studies Library, Central Library)

Salford has not, in general, attracted the same ethnic and cosmopolitan communities as Manchester, but the regeneration and redevelopment programmes that are taking place, especially in areas like Salford Quays, may change that situation within the next few years.

Life after Cotton in Salford

The decline of the cotton manufacturing industry and its attendant engineering industries hit Salford hard and its life blood began to ebb away, although towards the end of the 19th century industry in Salford had begun to diversify a little. Rainwear and waterproof clothing were manufactured in Broughton and, from 1880, rubber-covered cables. The Greengate and Irwell Rubber Co Ltd and W.T. Glover and Co Electrical Wire and Cable Makers in Salford also manufactured these items. Hogback Cars were situated in Pendleton and around 1904–05 the first Salford registered car appeared. John Shaw and Sons, Salford Ltd were hydraulic engineers, while Carver Walker were paper manufacturers.

Nevertheless, during the 20th century industry underwent major changes in Salford. Thousands were unemployed during the depression of the 1930s.

A depressing picture of how grim parts of Salford had become is best illustrated by a report from a 1931 survey by the Salford Women Citizens on housing conditions in St Matthias ward, described as one of the worst slums in Salford:

'*A district of large works and factories with high chimneys and overshadowing walls under which are huddled congested slum houses, mean streets, running at odd angles, designed only from the point of view of the most rigid economy of ground. Here and there is a narrow overhung passage twisting into a confined croft or court, or an ill-paved, badly drained, narrow alley, in which rubbish collects.*'

Many of the houses were rat infested. Most lacked elementary amenities and decencies and there were no open spaces for children to play in. Out of 950 houses visited by the Inspectors, 257 were found to be in a state of bad repair with leaking roofs, stripped plaster, broken flooring and rotten woodwork. Throughout the enquiry, the Inspectors were '*struck by the courage and perseverance with which the greater number of tenants kept their houses clean and respectable under most adverse conditions ... all honour is due to those brave housewives who, whilst waiting for better conditions are straining so hard to improve their present environment.*'

Coal mining had finished by 1939. Cotton manufacture had ceased by 1971. Brewing suffered the same fate. Whitbread Brewery was the only one left by 1972 and this is now closed. Berry Wiggins also closed their

A.R.O.E.
workers' buses
in Greengate in
1955.
(Manchester
Archives and
Local Studies
Library, Central
Library)

Lion
Foodpackers Ltd,
Cornbrook,
c.1948.
(Manchester
Archives and
Local Studies
Library, Central
Library)

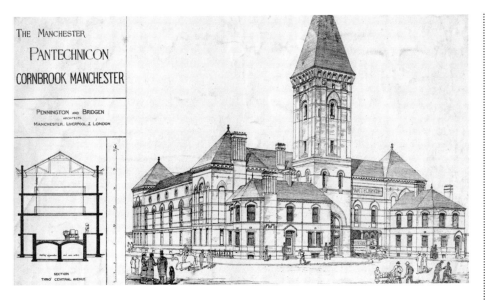

*Pantechnicon
Warehouses,
Cornbrook,
c.1878.
(Manchester
Archives and
Local Studies
Library, Central
Library)*

*Crow Carrying
Co., Greengate, in
1959. (Manchester
Archives and
Local Studies
Library, Central
Library)*

oil refinery by the Manchester Ship Canal in 1972. Between 1965–1991 nearly 50,000 jobs were lost in Salford, which amounted to a third of the available job total.

Wakes Week

The name 'wakes' originated from the Anglo-Saxon 'woeccan' and the Wakes Holiday developed out of the holy days celebrated by the church, although people also celebrated other high days important in the agricultural calendar, such as May Day, Midsummer and Harvest Home

Fire at A.V. Roe, Greengate, in 1960. (Manchester Archives and Local Studies Library, Central Library)

(Lughnasadh). Originally, 'wakes' was a religious festival, held to celebrate the day of the patron saint of the local church, so to each congregation their saint's day was viewed as the most important day of the year. The name 'wake' comes from the practice of staying awake all night to pray, on the eve of a saint's day. The term 'funeral wake' is from the same origin. By the 1800s the wakes had become a time of merrymaking, with fairs and dancing, eating and drinking to excess, but for the factory workers in the early 1800s these celebrations were out of reach. Long hours and bad working conditions meant that the wakes were just a childhood memory for most of them.

However, in the latter part of the 19th century and the first half of the 20th century, Wakes Weeks became common again, and by 1870 the idea of a week's holiday for factory workers, albeit unpaid, was beginning to be accepted. As it was more cost effective for the mill to shut down and give everyone a week off, it became usual for all the mills in one area to close together. Reviving the old name for celebrations, this became known as Wakes Week. The railways had opened up new vistas and the possibility of travel had become a reality for large numbers of workers as hours and conditions slowly improved towards the end of the 19th century. Desperate to escape from the mills to the open air and the countryside, and preferably the invigorating and cleansing atmosphere of the coast, seaside resorts became very popular with mill workers for their wakes holidays. Blackpool, with its miles of golden beaches, was particularly appealing. Families saved hard all year for their annual treat. Most could not afford hotels, choosing instead to stay in boarding houses. They were expected to provide their own food, which the landlady would cook for them, and there was an extra charge for use of the house cruet (salt and pepper). Determined to enjoy their one week of freedom, many people 'let their hair down' and 'let off steam' by doing outrageous, boisterous things that they would not dream of doing otherwise, and saucy postcards were sent to those left at home. Social expectations were very different then, however, and it was mostly good clean fun. There was a little of what might be termed mischief, but the vicious vandalism, the trashing of rooms, the wanton drunkenness and drug-taking of today were unknown.

Canterbury Hall, Salford Music Hall, in 1860. (Manchester Archives and Local Studies Library, Central Library)

Samuel Bamford, a Lancashire writer, has left a vivid word portrait of the wakes in his home town of Middleton during the early 19th century.

'*The first weekend was full of fairs and festivities, followed by sporting events at the beginning of the week; but by the Wednesday it was usually downhill all the way in a haze of alcohol until the end of the week when hangovers, and depression at the thought of the return to work, kicked in.*'

Salford in Modern Times

After the decline of the textile industry and the closure of the docks in the latter part of the 20th century, Salford became a city of contrasts with regenerated 'inner' areas like Salford Quays and the city centre standing cheek by jowl with some of the most socially deprived and violent areas in the country. 'Outer' areas like Swinton, Worsley and Walkden enjoy much better conditions and merge gradually into large tracts of attractive open countryside. Slum clearances of the last half a century have removed many of the endless rows of Victorian terraces, and Silk Street, Adelphi Street and Great Clowes Street have been built-up with huge blocks of flats to house people from the Greengate and Trinity wards. There are now around a quarter of a million people living in Salford, and over a third of Salford housing stock is council-owned. Regent Road, one of the main approaches to Salford, which was a busy road in 1916 and 1929 with houses, shops, the Regent Theatre (see Cross Street) and Assembly Rooms, is completely changed and mostly denuded. On Great Clowes Street stood the Victoria Theatre, which opened on 10 December 1900 and closed on 19 July 1958. From a theatre, it was converted to a cinema, then back to a theatre, then once again back to a cinema. The advent of television, however, hit the cinema industry hard. Salford Shopping Precinct has replaced the corner shops, which were once the 'lifeblood of the community'. The cobbled streets are mostly gone, replaced with smooth tarmac for the many more faster, sleeker vehicles than those of a hundred years ago. Only suicidal youngsters would play street games today.

In the 21st century the job emphasis has switched to road transport, with hire firms like Salford Van Hire doing good business; Stylo Plastics in the plastics industry; light industry and warehousing with estates at Ordsall and Brindle Heath; commercial and office blocks under new regeneration schemes like the West Riverside Scheme and, of course, Salford Quays, which is also a major tourist attraction.

Salford Rugby Club, formed in 1879, continues to flourish and Salford Reds (as they are known) now have an international reputation.

The first new bridge to be built in 100 years over the River Irwell between Manchester and Salford is the 'pointed biro pen' bridge, a footbridge that opened in September 1995. Dr Santiago Calatrava, a Spanish architect, won a competition with his design for the footbridge, which was built between Blackfriars Bridge and Albert Bridge and was known as the Calatrava Bridge to G.W.S. (God's Wonderful Salford!)

Coal and Canals

Coal and canal timeline in the Worsley area

1759 Work commences on Bridgewater Canal and navigable levels; engineered first by John Gilbert and then by James Brindley.

1776 Bridgewater Canal reaches Manchester.

1795 Extension of Bridgewater Canal to Leigh began.

1770 Navigable levels reach Walkden.

1776 Bridgewater Canal opened to Runcorn on 21 March.

1801 Navigable levels reach Buckley Lane.

1887 Last coal passes on navigable levels.

1968 Last sailing from Ellesmere Pit to Worsley Delph on 28 September.

1968 Last person to see navigable levels and leave by cage at Ellesmere Pit is John (Jack) Harrison of NCB, before shafts were infilled.

1968 All concrete stoppings at Ellesmere Pit were completed on 10 October.

1968 Last day of pumping from pits to navigable levels on 10 November.

1968 Filling in of the Ellesmere Pit main mining shaft (No. 2) is completed on 11 November.

1968 Closure of the navigable levels and Mosley Common colliery.

1999 Last inspection of the navigable levels.

Water Power

There were water-driven mills in Salford for milling corn and, from the end of the 18th century, for powering cotton mills. Mode Wheel Mill on the River Irwell and Kersal Mill below the mill pond on Singleton Brook are both examples of water-driven corn mills, while Ackers Mill on The Crescent and William Douglas's Mill at Pendleton were examples of water-driven cotton mills. The mills, especially the cotton mills, needed weirs on the river in order to get sufficient quantity and strength of water flow. The Mode Wheel weir on the Irwell was replaced by locks on the Manchester Ship Canal. As time went on the mills became steam-driven, like the Langworthy Brothers's mills, and took their water from the canals and rivers by prior agreement with the relevant water authority.

Waterways

By 1720 the Mersey and the Irwell were navigable and, in fact, there was an early quay on the Irwell at Salford almost oppoosit St Mary's Church.

The River Irwell and Salford Bank Mills in 1937. (Manchester Archives and Local Studies Library, Central Library)

After river improvements occasioned by competition from the canals during the latter part of the 18th century, passenger services to Runcorn and Liverpool sailed from a landing stage downstream from New Bailey Bridge. Originally, the Bridgewater Canal was due to terminate at Salford but the Manchester, Bolton and Bury Canal went down to the Irwell via a series of locks near Ordsall Lane, and from 1794 onwards narrow boats for transporting coal and cargoe barges served Salford. The Bridgewater Canal terminated at Castlefield instead. In 1894 the terminal docks for the Manchester Ship Canal were dug at Ordsall.

Corn millers were upset by the construction of locks and weirs because when the mill races allowed too much water to escape there was conflict with the barge men over low water levels. Water wheels were often given female names. Mode's Wheel was a derivative of Maud's Wheel. The surrounding area of Mode Wheel was still rural in the 1890s. At Mode Wheel '...the flour mill on the Salford bank also crushed logwood for the manufacture of dyes for the textile industry'. From 1806 onwards there were lock keepers. They lived in small white-washed cottages with a pentagonal porch, like a toll-house, so that they could watch for boats. It had proved necessary to employ keepers because of the increase in canal traffic and because of damage done to lock gates by boatmen.

Coal

The area was known for its rich seams of coal, which included thick seams in West Salford, the Irwell Valley, Pendleton Pit and around Worsley. Coal mining dates back to the 14th century in the Boothstown and Worsley areas. Until the end of the 17th-century mines were open-cast like shallow pits, which were known as Bell Pits. The main problem was that the seams, though there were plenty of them, were quite thin and had a pronounced slant downwards from north to south. The major problem with deeper mines were gases – which necessitated technology for ventilation – and water – which necessitated technology for pumping. In 1729 a drainage sough from Walkden to Worsley was constructed. It was 3,000ft long and ran underground for 1,800ft.

The Act that enabled the building of the Bridgewater Canal, from Booth's Bank to Worsley and then to Manchester, was passed in 1759. Construction of underground canals, or navigable levels, to run past the coal faces, were also begun in 1759. The entrance to the underground waterway complex was next to the Bridgewater Canal at The Delph in Worsley village. The tunnels were then extended north towards Walkden and other tunnels along coal seams were built at right angles to the main navigable level. New pits were also sunk to the depth of the main navigable level. The navigable levels also provided means of drainage from the coal seams and an extra source of water for the main

Bridgewater Canal, Worsley, near the Delph, c.1820. (Salford Local Studies Library)

Bridgewater Canal. In addition to his own considerable coal mining properties, extra coal mining rights were also acquired from Mr Clowes at Booth Hall by the Duke of Bridgewater in 1789.

The seam of coal, known as the Four Foot Seam, which ran from Boothstown to Worsley, was mined successfully because of its proximity to the Duke of Bridgewater's Canal. The Duke built his canal system (see Worsley) to enable coal to be transported direct from the coal face to the centre of the Manchester. The pit at Abbots Fold was linked by a horse tramway to the canal in 1764, which was extended to the Ellenbrook Pits in the 1840s. The success of the underground levels of canals and coal seams at Worsley was repeated at neighbouring Boothstown when the Chaddock Level, which extended 18,000ft from the Bridgewater Canal to the Chaddock Colliery and beyond to the Queen Anne Pit and the Henfold Pit, was constructed in about 1816. Chaddock and Abbots Fold closed in 1868 and there was no longer a trace of them on the 1894 OS map.

Women and children worked in the mines alongside the men. It was a desperately harsh life and the lines of premature ageing and despair could be seen in their faces. However, at Worsley, women and children under 12 were no longer required to work underground after 1841. Mining was hard and dirty work, often hazardous, and women and girls rolled up their skirts and tied them trouser fashion so that they would not catch on anything. Trousers for women were deemed disgusting and immoral beyond belief in Victorian England, nevermind the health and safety issues caused by skirts and crinolines, and young men would travel for miles to take a forbidden peak at these outlandish and unseemly creatures.

Coal: a strange and mysterious story

The Bolton Evening News, for 1 March 1876, related a strange story:

A collier named Thomas Baxter was found dead on Monday morning, under circumstances which leave no doubt that he lost his life in a very remarkable manner. Baxter was a collier, about 46 years old, residing at the Worsley end of Tyldesley, in a place known as the Delph, situate in Old-lane. Here there resided as his wife Jane Mann, the mother of his four children. He was a man of intemperate habits and doubtful character, being known as a night poacher.

About twelve o'clock on Saturday night, his mistress states, he returned home in a state of intoxication, and in a short time, left the house, as she supposed, to go into the back yard. He did not, however, return, and his sudden disappearance gave the woman considerable alarm. About eleven o'clock on Monday morning, Baxter's remains were found in a ditch by John Doncaster, of Streetgate, Little Hulton, who states he was bird catching at the time. The ditch, which is about a quarter of a mile from the residence of the deceased man, contained no water, and it divides the fence from the field. There was a serious wound on the right temple, probably caused by a blow from a large piece of coal, which the man had carried with him into the ditch, this being tightly grasped under his right arm. His huge pockets were also filled with coal.

It is conjectured that in returning from Gidlow Colliery, from whence he stole the coals, he missed his path in crossing the fields in the night time and fell into the ditch. Having been a poacher fully accounts for the extraordinary dimensions of Baxter's pockets. The circumstances surrounding his death are probably unparalleled.

Historical Miscellany of Salford

Market and Fair

On 4 June 1228 Henry III granted Salford a weekly market on Wednesdays and an annual fair on the 'eve, day and morrow of the Nativity of St Mary...' (7, 8 and 9 September). Traditionally, this is believed to have been held on land at the end of Chapel Street near Greengate, one of the original boundaries of old triangular Salford, which lay within Chapel Street, Gravel Lane and Greengate. Infilled triangular market places were common in the 13th century, and it is possible that the triangular basis was a remnant of the ninth-century Danish occupation since the Danes were known to use and establish triangular fields. Greengate was the hub of Salford and it was here on The Green in front of the Bull's Head that Bonnie Prince Charlie was blessed by Dr John Cousins on his epic march south, in 1745, to claim the English crown. It was here, too, in 1830, that John Wesley preached to a large assembled crowd. Today all the area of The Green has been covered by a large urban car park.

Bull's Head, Greengate

Legend has it that the Bull's Head received its license just five minutes after the one granted to the Seven Stars in Withy Grove (across the Irwell

The Bull's Head, from a drawing in 1780, closed as a pub in 1931. (Manchester Archives and Local Studies Library, Central Library)

The Bull's Head, 1875. (Manchester Archives and Local Studies Library, Central Library)

in Manchester) in 1356. Greengate was then pretty rural and stood facing the village green. On the green there stood a cross surmounted by a gilt crown. There were stocks at its base into which the local drunks were put as a punishment. Not far away stood the courthouse, which faced Gravel Lane. When the Collegiate College (now Chetham's Library) was built adjacent to the Cathedral Church of Manchester in 1426 it is said that the workmen would quench their thirst at the Bull's Head and that in summer the local clergy '...used to spend many a long bright evening in a game of bowls played on the green...'

The Bull's Head was a fine black and white timbered building of partial cruck construction and may well have been the original building of 1350. An engraving from 1780 shows a bear dancing outside the inn. It was the former town house of the Allan family and the cruck method of construction used in the building of the house could be clearly seen. There is no doubt that the Bull's Head was a popular hostelry and indeed the centre of much of Salford life prior to the Industrial Revolution. Until around 1900 other old cottages dating back to Tudor times surrounded the inn, but today the area is unrecognisable from early descriptions and mostly lies under a modern car park. The Bull's Head closed as a pub in 1931 and, after being badly damaged by fire in 1937, it was demolished.

The Bull's Head in Greengate, from 1900. (Manchester Archives and Local Studies Library, Central Library)

Old Licensed House, Greengate, a Tudor building that can no longer be seen today, c.1902.

Pearl Spring

Pearl Spring is first mentioned in 1511 and lay on the banks of the River Irwell between New Bailey Bridge and Irwell Street Bridge, and it seems to have been some kind of spa. It is possible that Salford was known locally to have a spa with healing waters (like the rather more famous Buxton in

Derbyshire) to which sick or disabled people were brought in the hope of a cure. Henry VIII's historiographer, John Leland, travelled the country describing what he saw for the king. Confirming that he believed it to be a spa, Leland wrote of the Pearl Spring in Salford:

'... a broket or pirle of water running out of an hill nere the toune, and cumming thorough a peace of the toune withyn the wall...creples were carried to the poul...and near was the spaw...'

(The 'spaw' being the spa house and Leland's description indicating how the Pearl Spring received its name.)

In Elizabeth Raffald's *Directory* of 1772 there was a cart road to the 'Pirle Spring' or 'Cold Bath' on the banks of the Irwell. The road branched off Chapel Street at the corner of Ordsall Lane and went along the line of Bolton Street (to the south of Bridge Street Bridge on the Manchester side – beyond the Edwardian pump house that now stands there) and possibly along Spaw (Spa) Street as well, but then it became just a footpath. The coming of the Industrial Revolution undoubtedly spelt the end for the Pearl Spring because, even if the spring had survived the onslaught of the mills, the water would have been so polluted it would have rendered it totally unfit for medicinal purposes.

Sacred Trinity Church

Sacred Trinity Church was founded by Humphrey Booth on Chapel Street in 1635 as a chapel of ease to Manchester Cathedral. Known then as the Chapel of Sacred Trinity, the original building was partly timber. However, this became unsafe due to the number of burials in the

Trinity Chapel. Salford. 1741.

Sacred Trinity Church, originally built in 1634 and the only church in Britain with the dedication of 'Flat Iron Church'. (Manchester Archives and Local Studies Library, Central Library)

surrounding marshy ground and it was demolished in 1750. Two years
later it was rebuilt from stone to an unprepossessing design. The tower
was still the original tower, in which six bells were hung in 1748, but the
tower was partly rebuilt in 1855. A flat iron market was held in front of
the church for a number of years. It is the only church in Britain with the
dedication of 'Flat Iron Church.'

Humphrey Booth, who lived at Booth Hall just off Greengate, also
endowed a charity to aid 'the poor, aged, needy or impotent Salfordians'
by allotting rents from a barn, meadows and pasture, which he had
bought in Piccadilly, Manchester. The charity still survives and funds
housing estates like Humphrey Booth Gardens for senior citizens.

Flat Iron Market

The Flat Iron Market was held on land around Holy Trinity Church (built
in 1635) and took its name from the shape of the piece of land on which
it was held. The Flat Iron Market closed in 1939. The *Manchester
Guardian* of 26 May 1906 records what it was like:

Photographs of the Iron Market on Chapel Street in 1894. (Manchester Archives and Local Studies Library, Central Library)

'...*everyone in Manchester knows the Flat Iron market, and a very large number do their fancy shopping there by night. The market is the hunting-park of the bargain hunters who want, or think they want, or imagine that they may some day want, a rusty old cavalry sword, or a pair of skates, or a bunch of curtain rings, or a pair of half-wellington boots, or a toy engine, or a bank of cord, green or red, or a little round looking-glass, or a pair of cork soles, or a bunch of old keys, or an old rusty lock, or a pink ice-cream, or a handful of hot chestnuts, or a small but cheerfully coloured copy of The Angelus - for a penny. You can even buy a policeman's helmet. Two heroes got one each, and after buttoning their jackets up to the chin ran through the market like a brace of Merry Andrews, startling timorous merchants by suddenly popping their helmeted heads round the corners of the stall.*

I think I should like to do all my marketing in the Flat Iron, for it is a real market, a place where you can swagger aloof if it suits your mind, or you can rub shoulders with the best of company, stopping occasionally to pass old-fashioned chaff..and when you stop to buy you plunge immediately into the old primeval realities of commerce. Here you do not stand sourly while a pale-faced short-tempered shopman whirls your purchase into a dexterously twisted screw of pale brown paper and sends your money trundling in a globe along naked wires. No; here before you

make a purchase you can slap and thump a thing, and abuse and sneer at it, and the man behind the stall will slap and thump it too, and praise it; and at last you'll get the price down to near to what he will take and you will give...I did not know, till I was told, that this market takes its name from its shape. The larger priced things, like clothes and oilcloth, are sold by Dutch auction...if you go to the market for pleasure only, when tired of hearing others bargain and chaff among the flare lamps you can cross the road to where the merry-go-rounds are whirling. Also sometimes there is a boxing booth, and there are several kinds of throwing games, one where you hurl balls at strangely whiskered dolls, which fall over backwards like life itself if you hit them fair...'

Adelphi

In 1740 the Adelphi District was known as '...Bank...Whitecross Bank; Bank Parade; Bank Place; and Salford Hospital which stood by the gate at the end of the road...' Salford ford led into Broughton from Greengate. Today the Adelphi/Bexley Square Conservation Area, to give it its full modern title, lies along the A6 corridor and is centered on the 18th century St Philip's Church, Salford's 'Hidden Gem'. It is bounded by Adelphi Street, Clemminson Street, East Market Street and Chapel Street and includes the Grade II listed properties of St Philip's, the Cathedral Church of St John the Evangelist, the Cathedral House on Chapel Street, the education offices, Salford Town Hall, the former County Court (now converted to luxury apartments) and some 18th-century houses in

Encombe Place close to the former Salford Royal Hospital complex. Salford Town Hall was built in 1827 and enlarged in 1844, after its purchase in 1834 by the Salford Commissioners constituted by the Act of 1829. The Commissioners, who were self-appointed, had replaced the Portmote in 1795. Originally, they were joint commissioners of Salford and Manchester but had become separate authorities in 1809.

Cross Lane

Cross Lane, which had junctions with Regent Road, Trafford Road, Eccles New Road and Trafford Lane, was one of the busiest thoroughfares. It had theatres at each end, barracks, the Stowell Memorial Church (built in 1869 in memory of the Revd Hugh Stowell,

Cross Lane, Salford, 1820–1825. (Salford Local Studies Library)

who had spent 40 years preaching in Salford before dying in 1865), markets to which cattle were driven, the Cattle Market Hotel and the Ship Inn, a notorious drinking den. At the junction with Eccles New Road there was a 'grand union' junction of tramlines laid in the cobbles: two lines turning right and left from each direction and two lines going straight across. Today this junction is in Crich Tramway Museum. At the Regent Road end of Cross Lane lay the Regent Theatre (opened in 1895 and burned down in 1941), where Houdini performed in 1904, escaping from a locked coffin, and at the other end of the street, the Windsor Bridge and Cross Lane Hippodrome Theatre, later the Windsor Theatre (opened in 1904 and closed down in 1956). A MacDonald's drive-thru now stands on the site. There was also Oliver Heywood's obelisk, which is the only feature of the theatre remaining today. Oliver Heywood was a philanthropic banker who helped Salford's poor and needy.

Bexley Square

It is ironic that Chapel Street, which became the first built-up area of new industrial Salford, should also become the first Salford slum. As Chapel Street declined in importance as the hub of Salford, Bexley Square became the new centre. The Town Cross having been removed, the Town Hall was built here and named after Lord Bexley, Chancellor of the Duchy of Lancaster, when he laid the Town Hall foundation stone in 1825. The Town Hall eventually became the court house. Just beyond this lies the Roman Catholic Cathedral of St John the Evangelist on Chapel Street.

The now disused Manchester and Salford Savings Bank and Peel Park Inn.

Nearby are the closed and shuttered buildings of the Manchester and Salford Savings Bank and the Peel Arms public house, while round the corner and set back from the road is St Philip's Church with its curiously proportioned round clock tower.

Salford Cathedral

The Cathedral Church of St John the Evangelist in Salford, designed by

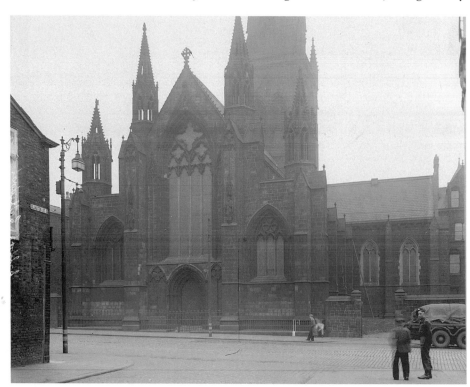

Matthew Hadfield, was built in 1844–1848 but not consecrated until 1890 after its building debts had been paid in full. The design of the church drew inspiration from other churches for some of its features and these included Howden Church in Yorkshire (West Door); the Abbey Church in Selby (choir and sanctuary); St Jacques at Liège (groined roof) and Newark Church (steeple). The Cathedral has a white marble altar, clean, high arches and a huge stained-glass window of the saints at the east end. Someone once wrote, with feeling, the following words:

*Salford
Cathedral as it is
today.*

*'...Cathedrals are built not only of steel and stone. They rise out of the
sacrifices and endeavours of many generations...'*

St Philip's Church, St Philip's Place

The church, which stands between Salford Cathedral and Salford Royal
Hospital, was designed in neo-Classical Greek style by Robert Smirke in
1825 and is unique in Salford. It has a bow-fronted porch with an ionic
colonnade, a balustraded parapet and a bell tower with a clock face. In
1962 the church became St Philip's after St Stephen's Church on nearby
St Stephen's Street closed and the two congregations merged.

*Opposite: St
Philip's Church
designed by
Robert Smirke in
the neo-classical
style and built in
1825, in 1900
and the present
day (over the
page).*

Salford Royal Infirmary

The hospital was built in 1830, an extension was added in 1911 and it stood close to Salford Cathedral, at the corner of Oldfield Road and Chapel Street, opposite the Boer War memorial. Superceded by the enlarged Hope Hospital in Pendleton, the old hospital building lay empty for years but it has now been converted into the Royal Apartments with luxury home sharing ownership facilities.

The Salford Royal Hospital, now converted to the Royal Apartments, and how it looked in 1892 (below).

Salford Library

The Salford Library was founded in 1849, a year before the Public Libraries Act of 1850, and named the Royal Museum and Library. It opened in January 1850 and was the first free municipal library in the country. Charles Dickens described the new library as '...a great free school...' from which the working classes would benefit greatly. The library was situated within Lark Hill mansion on the Lark Hill estate, which was purchased by public subscription in 1846. The grounds were turned into a public park for, as Edmund Potter put it, the 'newly leisured classes', and named Peel Park after Sir Robert Peel (1788-1850), who had been instrumental in the recent repeal of the Corn Laws. The library still stands on the site of Lark Hall Mansion, adjacent to the Peel Building, which is part of the University of Salford. The art gallery and museum are also housed within the library building as well as the Salford Local History Studies Library. The art gallery held a large collection of paintings by L.S. Lowry until they were moved to the new purpose-built gallery at the Lowry Centre. A central feature of the museum is Lark Hill Place, which is a recreation of a typical Victorian street.

Working Class Movement Library

Jubilee House on Salford Crescent, opposite the public library, houses the Working Class Movement Library, whose aim is to '...promote the

The Salford Library in 1958. (Manchester Archives and Local Studies Library, Central Library)

The Salford Library doorway in 1973.

Peel Park Museum and art gallery in 1880. (Manchester Archives and Local Studies Library, Central Library)

Peel Park in Salford, 2004, still a public park.

education of the public in relation to the history of the working class movement by facilitating and promoting research and dissemination of information about all aspects of such history...' The library has a large collection of books, pamphlets, journals, manuscripts and ephemera, dating from 1760 onwards, of labour history material, which includes: '...politics of all shades, economic history, trade unionism, co-operation, social conditions, education, agriculture and the women's movement, also

The Working Class Movement Library in Jubilee House on Salford Cresent.

local histories, reports of trials, biographies and autobiographies, novels on social themes and working class plays, poetry and songs…' amassed by Edmund and Ruth Frow, both active trades unionists.

The Working Class Movement Library, the result of the Frow's hard work since the 1960s, was opened at Jubilee House in 1987 by Frank Allaun, then MP for Salford East. The library holds materials on the Amalgamated Engineering Union; the Amalgamated Machine, Engine and Iron Grinders and Glaziers Society; Amalgamated Society of Engineers; Amalgamated Union of Building Trade Workers; Amalgamated Society of Wire Drawers and Kindred Workers; the Boilermakers' Society; Draftsmen's Union; Typographical Society; Foundry Workers' Union; Amalgamated Association of Card and Blowing Room Operatives; Ship Constructors Aid Shipwrights Association; Amalgamated Weavers' Association, National Union of General and Municipal Workers and the National Society of Drillers; Peterloo; the Spanish Civil War (including the Foodship records) and a host of other records.

Salford University

The Salford Working Men's College (founded in 1858) and the Pendleton Mechanics Institute (founded in1850) combined in 1896 to become the Salford Technical Institute, which stood on the campus on The Crescent. Funded by local manufacturers and mill owners, these institutes had direct links to local industries. In 1908 Salford Technical Institute underwent further changes and split into two colleges: the Royal College of Advanced Technology and the other Peel Park Technical College. The opening of the Royal College was attended by the Duke and Duchess of York, later to become King George V and Queen Mary. The chief

The Salford Technical Institute in Peel Park, c.1910.

The front of the current Peel Park Campus, University of Salford.

industries in Salford at that time were mechanical engineering, chemical works, textiles and construction, which influenced the choice of courses on offer. The Royal College in turn became the University of Salford in 1967 with HRH The Duke of Edinburgh being its first chancellor. Peel Park Technical College became Salford Technical Institute in 1961, Salford College of Technology in 1970 and University College Salford in 1992. Finally, in 1996, the University of Salford merged with University College (which stood on Frederick Road) to form the present campus. Today the University has about 18,000 students from all over the world in its 14 schools and 13 research institutes.

*Part of Salford
University beside
the River Irwell.*

*Exchange Station,
Salford, c.1905.
(Salford Local
Studies Library)*

Exchange Station

Salford station opened in 1838 as the terminus and head office of the
Manchester, Bolton and Bury Railway Company. The station was linked
to Victoria Station in Manchester by a bridge crossing New Bailey Street
and became known as the Salford mainline station, although its approach
lay in Manchester.

Salford Baths

Collier Street Public Baths (named after a hardworking Methodist
Minister named Samuel Francis Collier) were opened by Manchester and
Salford Baths and Laundry Company Inc. in 1855. It was usual for public
baths to offer facilities for both bathing and the washing and drying of
clothes and bedding, since many workers cottages had either grossly

inadequate facilities or none at all. This remained common practice until after World War One. The Baths closed in 1880 when Salford Corporation opened their own Baths on Blackfriars Street. The men's pool was larger and more ornate than the ladies' pool. An unusual feature of the Baths were the laminated wooden roof arches. The Baths closed in the early 20th century and later became a matchbox factory. During World War Two an air raid shelter was built in the deep end of the former ladies' pool.

Salford Pals

The Salford Pals are '…four unsung Fusilier Battalions…' of the British Expeditionary Forces in France and Flanders during World War One and afterwards (1914–19). They started as the 1st, 2nd, 3rd, and 4th Salford Pals, then, as events altered the character of each Battalion, they became the 15th, 16th, 19th and 20th Lancashire Fusiliers as the war took a heavy toll on the original Salford Brigade members. There is a memorial to earlier Fusiliers from 1905 in Salford Royal Hospital.

The Drill Hall of the 3rd Battalion Lancashire Fusiliers, c.1896.

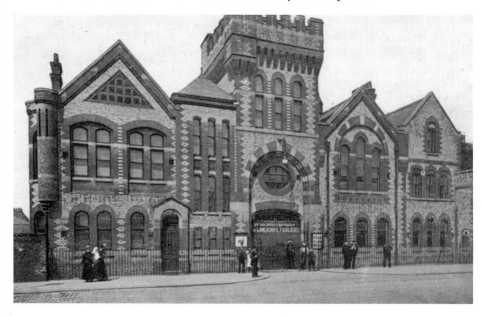

Boer War Memorial

The memorial stands on the green roundabout at the junction of Oldfield Road with the A6 and commemorates those who fell in the South African war against the Boers in 1899-1902. It was unveiled by King Edward VII and Queen Alexandra on 13 July 1905. The inscription reads:

South Africa 1899-1902
Volunteer Active Service Companies of the Royal Lancashire Fusiliers
'daring in all things'

Phillips and Lee Mill

This was an early cotton mill, which stood between Chapel Street and the River Irwell. It was built in 1798 and constructed, unusually for the time, of cast-iron pillars and beams. By 1806 the mill had gas lighting and used some of their gas supply to light some of Chapel Street as well. Phillips and Lee Mill was destroyed by bombs during the Blitz in World War Two.

Salford Gas Works

Chapel Street in Salford became the first street in the world to be lit by gas, supplied from a nearby mill. Salford Gas Works and its administration offices were housed in an imposing and somewhat ornate building, completed in 1819 on Bloom Street next to Salford Model Lodging House. In 1887 Superintendent Samuel Hunter disappeared with the Gas Works' takings and profits, closely followed by the then chief executive. The affair became known to posterity as the Salford Gas Scandal.

Crooked Billet concert room in 1850. (Manchester Archives and Local Studies Library, Central Library)

Salford gas meter inspectors in 1917. (Manchester Archives and Local Studies Library, Central Library)

The former Gas Works, completed in 1819 and situated on Bloom Street.

Salford Model Lodging House

The lodging house stood on Bloom Street next to the Gas Works. The house could sleep 100 itinerant workers, giving them clean beds and safe shelter for the night. The building later became a nursery and was then converted into flats for young people.

Museum of Coal Mining at Buile Hill

Buile Hill was designed in neo-Classical style by James Barry and built in

1825–1827. Unusually, there is a covered carriage port, which was known as a 'port-cochère'. The house was later extended by Edward Walters (who designed the Free Trade Hall in Manchester). Past residents include Sir Thomas Potter, the first Mayor of Manchester, and his son, John, who was MP for Manchester. Both men were part of the large family from which Beatrix Potter, the internationally acclaimed children's writer, came. The house, together with 80 adjoining acres, was bought by Salford Corporation in 1902. Four years later it opened as a Museum of Natural History and remained a museum until the 1950s. In 1959, as part of a joint enterprise with the National Coal Board, excavations took place

Buile Hall, now the museum of coal mining, designed in neo-classical style by James Barry.

and Buile Hill No.1 Pit was constructed in the basement of the house. Subsequently, a drift pit was reconstructed on the ground floor. Dry rot forced closure in the 1970s, but eventually Buile Hill reopened in 1979.

Imperial War Museum North

The museum, which is part of The Lowry complex in Salford, offers an unusual and unique insight into the meaning of war. The building is designed as three shards of a shattered globe, representing air, earth and water, symbolising the way in which war devastates the world. The land shard is the largest and has six war time lines: 1900–14; 1914–18; 1919–38; 1939–45; 1946–90; 1990–present plus half a dozen special exhibitions featuring different aspects of war.

The showpieces of the museum are its three 'Big Picture Shows' entitled 'Why War?', 'Weapons of War', and 'Children and War', during which '…over sixty projectors throw images on to twenty screens, some of them five metres high…' The result is that visitors suddenly find themselves surrounded by war, with all its drama, fear, tragedy and destruction. In a dim half light, images of bombed streets and houses, rescuers clawing at rubble, fields of poppies and children in gas masks flash on to the walls and the noise of whining sirens, gunfire, explosions and fighter planes overhead drowns the reality of peaceful everyday life. It is an emotional and sobering experience and the audience sees, hears and learns more about war during 15 minutes than most of them will experience in a lifetime.

The Imperial War Museum North proclaims that it is '…a war museum with a heart…' and it is impossible to remain unmoved or indifferent to the way in which it portrays the reality of war.

Halls of Salford

There were a number of Halls in Salford and its townships, some of which still exist and some of which have been demolished.

Agecroft Hall

On the edge of Kersal Moor stood Agecroft Hall. The name originates form 'edge croft', a croft being a field in which the bleaching and drying of cloth was carried out. The earliest deed for this 'bleaching field on the edge' of the moor is dated 1199, in which King John granted the 'bleaching field' to Elias de Peneburi along with the village of Pendlebury. In 1291 the Prestwich family bought Edgecroft or Agecroft Hall and Pendlebury lands from the de Peneburi family. The estates then passed by marriage to the Langleys in 1350. The family enlarged Agecroft Hall in Tudor times so that it contained 50 rooms.

In 1561 Anne Langley inherited the hall and the Pendlebury demesne, as well as Prestwich water mill and pasture lands on Swinton Moor. She married William Dauntesey and Agecroft passed into the hands of the Dauntesey family, who held it until 1813 when it was inherited by their maternal cousins, the Rucks. By 1920 Agecroft Hall was surrounded by collieries, canals and railways and left empty, so was in a state of decay. However, in 1925 Thomas Williams and his wife, an American couple, saw the place and liked it. Mr Williams bought Agecroft Hall and had it dismantled, brick by brick, and shipped to Richmond, Virginia, where it still stands today.

Brick Hall

The Brick Hall was built in about 1760 by the Duke of Bridgewater for his agents. Previously, agents had lived at Worsley Old Hall. It was so called because it was built entirely of locally manufactured bricks and was said to have a 'splendid profile'. The Brick Hall also became a centre of local administration for the Duke's canals. It was demolished in 1846, just over 80 years after it was built.

Drywood Hall

The hall was the home of the Massey family and stood on Worsley Road. Rebuilt at the end of the 19th century, it is now the Bridgewater School.

Hazelhurst Hall

Stood to the east of Drywood Hall, Hazelhurst Hall was the home of the Lomax family. The later 18th-century part of the hall still exists as a farm, but an older, lower building was demolished in around 1949.

Hope Hall

Hope Hall was built in mediaeval times and then rebuilt around 1750 by Daniel Bayley. T.B. Bayley (d.1803) carried out farming experiments and wrote a number of reports. Later, further additions were made to the hall, but it was finally demolished in 1956. The name is commemorated in nearby Hope Hospital.

Kempnough Hall

Built in the 14th century with 15th-century additions, the hall stands on Roe Green, west of Kempnough Hall Road. This is a black and white timbered building on a stone base with a slate roof and brick chimneys, restored and renovated in 1977. The Kempnough estate was first recorded in the early 13th century, but by the 15th century was being referred to as Kempnall. The hall was let at an annual rent of two shillings, which remained unchanged over the centuries. Today the hall is divided into three houses.

Kenyon Hall, Little Hulton, (Kenyon Peel Hall or Old Peel Hall)

A black and white half-timbered building on a low stone base, built in around 1630 and demolished in 1957, it was the seat of the Kenyon family. Bungalows and Our Lady of Lancashire Martyr's Church now stand on the site.

Kersal Hall

In 1590 Kersal Moor was called the Common or Kersal Wood. In 1697

Kersal Wood ('...now or late called Kersal Moor'), covering approximately 100 acres, was apportioned equally between James Chetham of Turton, Henry Greenhaulgh of Brandsome and Edward Byrom of Manchester. Sometime before 1616 the manor of Kersal was divided between the Syddall, Chetham and Ravald families. Kersal Hall was, therefore, not really the manor house. It stood on the corner of Littleton Road and Moor Road; a typical Tudor black and white timbered building built by William Lever of Darcy Lever for his family in the early 1540s. Sadly the hall has not survived; it was demolished in 1937.

Peel Hall
The original mediaeval moated hall known as Wicheaves was held by the Hultons and the Tyldesleys before being rebuilt by the Mort family during the 17th century. The second hall was built from stone with two wings and had three gables to the front. Sold to the Fletchers in the 19th century, it was rebuilt again in 1840. It was used as a hospital in the 20th century and became a Grade II listed building. It was finally demolished in 1996 as it had become structurally unsafe.

Wardley Hall
Wardley, or Wordelegh as it was known in 1292, stood on lands that had belonged to the Knights Hospitallers. The Tyldesley family held the Hall from 1420 to the mid-16th century, when they sold it, together with its water mill and several hundred acres, after being rebuilt in 1533, to Gilbert Sherington. Thurstan de Tyldesley was one of the last Tyldesleys to live there. Roger Downes bought the hall in 1609 and farmed sheep. Wardley Hall was a moated hall built around a quadrangle and it had 19 hearths; not a cheap place to run in the days when there was a tax on hearths. The Great Hall, which had an open-timbered roof, still survives. It was later sold to the Savages and the Barrys (1734). The then daughter of the house, Penelope Cholmondley, sold the hall and its estate to Francis, 3rd Duke of Bridgewater, in 1760 and became part of his growing estate. Today the hall is home to successive Bishops of Salford, after it was refurbished in 1900; but a golf course, cemetery and housing estate occupy its once spacious lands.

Wharton Hall
Built during the 16th century, it stood on Wharton Lane, south of Wharton Chapel. It was described as a '...two storey farmhouse of brick and timber and plaster construction...' The hall was held by the Whartons until 1587, then the Asshetons and by the Mort family from around 1650. It was demolished in the 1950s.

Worsley Old Hall within the City of Salford, from a postcard c.1905.

Worsley Old Hall

Built by the Masseys in the 15th century, the hall was a black and white timbered and red brick house with a slate roof. It lies west of Walkden Road between the A580.

After the demolition of Hulme Hall in Manchester in 1845, some fine wooden carvings from the hall were sent to Worsley Old Hall. No one knows why they were sent to Worsley or what these carvings represented, but there were rumours that they were supposed to be likenesses of demons that the Dowager Lady Prestwich had conjured to guard hidden treasure that she had buried in the grounds of Hulme Hall during the Civil War (1640–9). Lancashire and Cheshire Antiquarian Society members visited Worsley Old Hall on Saturday 7 October 1899 to inspect these carvings and the following is a description written by one of their number:

'*...the old oak carvings are carefully preserved in Lady Ellesmere's sitting-room, and consists of a series of spirited, grotesque, and allegorical heads with an intermixture of ornamental devices, in oaken panels, brought early in the present century from one of the Staterooms of Hulme Hall, Manchester. Many of the sculptured heads represent the domestic buffoons of the sixteenth century, to which period this sculpture is to be referred. Others are suggested by the religious mysteries which formed in early times such inexhaustible subjects for the painter and sculptor. These heads much resemble those carved images seen so frequently in the choirs of ecclesiastical buildings. The costumes appears to be mostly of the reign on Henry VII and Henry VIII. One of the panels represents the eagle and child, the Stanley crest...*'

The present hall is of a later date; some 17th century but mostly 19th and 20th century. The 17th-century, vaulted cellars are used as a banqueting hall and much of the original demesneland continues to be farmed today.

Worsley New Hall

Lord Francis Egerton, the great nephew of the 3rd Duke of Bridgewater, who inherited Worsley, built Worsley New Hall, a 'great Gothic mansion', between 1840–6, at a cost of £41,000. During the construction, some of the wooden carvings from Hume Hall (demolished in 1845) said to be of 'unearthly spirits' were incorporated into the New Hall. Queen Victoria and Prince Albert stayed there in 1852 and so did King Edward VII and Queen Alexandra in 1909. The hall became a military hospital during World War One and was used by the military during World War Two. It was demolished between 1946–9.

Ordsall Hall

Images of Ordsall Hall in 1840 and 1900, the latter showing it in a dilapidated state. (Manchester Archives and Local Studies Library, Central Library)

Ordsall Hall is a romantic, black and white timbered building, which stands in the middle of a large, green meadow with rowan trees growing close by. For a moment there is a brief time slip, but the painted iron railings and security cameras are a reminder that the hall is no longer a Tudor idyll but a 21st century anachronism, sandwiched between a modern housing development and an industrial estate. Progress, though, cannot rob the hall of its essence or the history that has soaked into its walls over the centuries. However, Erasmus stayed there in 1499 and painted a less than pretty picture:

'...the floors are made of clay and are covered with layers of rushes, constantly replenished, so that the bottom layer remains for 20 years harbouring spittle, vomit, the urine of dogs and men, the dregs of beer, the remains of fish and other nameless filth...'

It is a description which might make even Rentokil go pale, but there was no Health and Safety Executive in the 15th century.

Ordsall Hall from a postcard c.1900.

The first mention of 'Ordeshala' comes in 1177, when feudal dues were paid. The name comes from old English 'halh', meaning a nook, and 'Ord', meaning a sword, point or a ridge of land. Ord's Nook has a cosy ring to it and it seems likely that there was already a house at Ordsall as early as 1251, when William Ferrers, Earl of Derby, exchanged the manor for estates in Pendleton.

However, Ordsall was the seat of the Radclyffe family for over 300 years, from 1335 until 1662, and this was the important period in its history. Sir John de Radclyffe, whose motto was 'Caen, Crecy, Calais' (a testament to his military service), inherited the moated manor house with its woods and fields in 1354. The deeds showed that he was master of '...a messauge, 120 acres of land, 12 acres of meadow and 12 acres of wood...'

Sir John had fought alongside Edward III (1327–1377) in the French wars and, like Edward, he had been impressed with the skills of the Flemish weavers. When the king asked him if there was any further reward he would like in return for his valour on the battlefield, Sir John

Ordsall Hall, present day.

requested permission to take a small number of Flemish weavers with him when he returned to Ordsall. His request was readily granted and Sir John built cottages on the edge of his estate to house his newly acquired weavers.

The Flemish were highly skilled in weaving wool, silk and fustian and they passed on their skills to their English neighbours. This was to form the foundation of the English textile industry and the Cottonopolis boom of the 19th century. Even by Tudor times Manchester was known for its 'smallwares' (ribbons, braids, laces, garters etc) and its 'Manchester cottons' (a napped woollen weave).

Sir John, and his son, Richard, enlarged Ordsall Hall and by 1380 it had '...a hall, five chambers, a kitchen and a chapel [licensed in 1361]...'

Salford Woollen Works, 1836. (Manchester Archives and Local Studies Library, Central Library)

as well as '...two stables, three granges [home farms], two shippons [cattle sheds], a garner [granary], a dovecote, an orchard and a windmill...' The large cruck hall was replaced with the Great Hall by Sir Alexander Radclyffe, High Sheriff of Lancashire, in 1512. His great-granddaughter, Margaret Radclyffe, was a favourite Maid of Honour to Queen Elizabeth I, although it is said that Margaret died of a broken heart in 1599 after her twin brother, Alexander, was lost at sea.

After John Radclyffe was forced to sell Ordsall Hall in 1662, as a result of financial hardship suffered through his father supporting the Royalists in the Civil War (1640-49), it had a chequered history. It was owned by the Egerton family of Tatton from 1758 until 1959 and they rented it to a succession of tenants. By the end of the 19th century Ordsall was surrounded by the grimness of the millscapes and had lost a lot of its former glory. In 1875 Haworth's Mill rented the hall for use as a Working Men's Club, offering gymnasium facilities, billiards, a skittle alley and a bowling green. It was an ironic fate, perhaps, in view of the fact that a long dead owner had been responsible for the introduction of the textile industry to the north-west.

However, since 1959 the hall has belonged to Salford Corporation, who have undertaken a great deal of work to restore it and it is now a museum. This does not detract in any way from seeing the hall as it once was and wandering through the restored rooms still exercises the imagination of past times and events at Ordsall.

The former Great Hall, measuring 42ft in length by 25ft in width (according to Frank Hird in *Lancashire Stories*, 1913), has lost the temporary partitions effected by former tenants and has been restored to the black and white timbered room it once was. At the western end are three doors. The left hand door leads to the buttery, the central door to the kitchens and the right hand door to the pantry and bread store. The back and front doors of the Great Hall had screens to prevent draughts, and the front screen is still in situ. There is a narrow 'screens passage' between the doors and the screens. All that is missing is a member of the Radclyffe family hosting a dinner for family and friends around a long wooden table with the ale flowing freely and a feast of dishes unfamiliar to 21st century tastes.

Leading off the Great Hall is the Star Chamber, the oldest part of the building. This and the solar above are the only surviving section of the 14th-century manor house. To step into the Star Chamber is to step back in time. So called because of the lead stars on the ceiling placed there by an early Tudor craftsman, the Star Chamber is dark and quiet. So quiet it is as though the atmosphere was silent. A gilt frieze of early design runs around three sides of the ceiling. There is an '...*old wide chimney-piece, and in the right hand corner a small door that once opened upon a secret passage leading to a staircase in the chimney, which communicated with a little chapel, and hiding places in the roof...'* (Frank Hird. *Lancashire Stories*, 1913), but the windows and outer doors are not the originals.

It was here, in the Star Chamber, according to the popular legend immortalised in Harrison Ainsworth's novel *Guy Fawkes*, that Robert Catesby and Guy Fawkes hatched the Gunpowder Plot in 1605. In the days of James I a window in the Star Chamber overlooked a winding country lane from Oldfield. The solar above the Star Chamber was said to have been Guy Fawkes's bedroom and there was '....another small door opening to a secret passage in the 15ft square chimney and connected with the one from the lower floor...'

This street name commemorates the legend that the gunpowder plot was hatched at Ordsall Hall, which is situated nearby.

Although never proved, it is entirely possible that the Gunpowder Plot was hatched at Ordsall Hall. The Radclyffes were a Catholic family (and heavily fined for it) and acquaintances of Catesby's family, who were prominent Northamptonshire Catholics. Catesby was in deep trouble having been involved in a rebellion led by the Earl of Essex against Queen Elizabeth I and he had also been accused of trying to poison the Queen, both treasonable acts. Life was uncomfortable and dangerous for him in London, and Ordsall Hall offered him sanctuary at a safe distance from London. There is often a grain of truth in folklore and it is probable that Guy Fawkes did indeed stay at Ordsall Hall. There is no evidence that Sir John Radclyffe, who owned the Hall at the time, knew anything of the Gunpowder Plot and little reason why he should have known of the desperate whisperings that took place in the old quiet Star Chamber.

In Harrison Ainsworth's novel of 1835, Guy Fawkes fell in love with Viviana Radclyffe, who was later tortured to try and make her reveal the secrets of the Gunpowder Plot. This is almost certainly a fiction since there was no member of the Radclyffe family named Viviana and the Gunpowder Plot was discovered in London. The only contemporary Radclyffe women at Ordsall were Margaret, who had died in 1599, and Jane, aged around 30 in 1605, who was married to Sir Ralph Constable. That is not to say that Guy Fawkes could not, or did not, fall in love with Jane Radclyffe.

A passage in the novel tells of a perilous flight through Salford for Guy and Viviana and perhaps gives a rare glimpse of what life in pre-industrial Salford might have been like:

'*...after much debate, it was decided that their safest plan would be to proceed to Manchester, where Humphrey Chetham undertook to procure them safe lodgings at the Seven Stars, - an excellent hostel, kept by a worthy widow, who, he affirmed, would do anything to serve him. Accordingly, they set out at nightfall, - Viviana taking her place before Guy Fawkes, and relinquishing Zayda to the young merchant and the priest. Shaping their course through Worsley, by Monton Green and Pendleton, they arrived in about an hour within sight of the town, which then, - not a tithe of its present size, and unpolluted by the smoky atmosphere in which it is now constantly enveloped, - was not without some pretensions to a picturesque appearance ...crossing Salford Bridge, they mounted Smithy Bank, as it was then termed, and proceeding along Cateaton Street and Hanging Ditch, struck into Whithing (now Withy) Grove, at the right of which, just where a few houses were beginning to straggle up Shude Hill, stood, and still stands, the comfortable hostel of the Seven Stars. Here they stopped, and were warmly welcomed by its buxom mistress, Dame Sutcliffe. Muffled in Guy Fawkes' cloak, the priest gained the chamber, to which he was ushered unobserved. And Dame Sutcliffe, though her Protestant notions were a little scandalized at her dwelling being made the sanctuary of a Popish priest, promised, at the instance of Master Chetham, whom she knew to be no favourer of idolatry in a general way, to be answerable for his safety...*'

There is also a legend that Guy Fawkes fled from troopers at Ordsall Hall, via secret subterranean passages, to a public house in Withy Grove in Manchester. Underground passages from the Hall to Manchester did exist as in April 1900 a letter published in the *Manchester Guardian* stated:

'*...I was shown a door in Hanging Bridge Hotel cellar where the arches could be seen and a door made up...it was the entrance to an underground passage under the Irwell...to...Ordsall Hall...the owner* had not traversed the passage himself, but the previous owner had, but had to turn back because of bad smells...'

Manchester Notes and Queries for 1901 published the following fragment:

'...when the licensed house at the Cathedral end of Hanging Bridge...was rebuilt, a tunnel was found with five or six skeletons with fragments of clothing and copper coin with Latin inscription...'

The coinage was said to be copper and probably dated from the reign of the Catholic Queen Mary Tudor (1553–8).

In Harrison Ainsworth's novel, Woden's Cave stood near the hall and played an important part in the story of Guy Fawkes. Although the name is reflected in Woden's Lane, which took its name from the Woden's Ford that had stood close to nearby Hulme Hall, there is no trace of this cave today. However, an old gentleman writing for *Lancashire Stories* in 1913 tells of how the countryside around Ordsall looked in the 1840s:

'...from Ordsall Lane the land to the west sloped upwards, and the outer entrance to the cave formed a pretty bay overshadowed by trees and shrubs...in the cave there was a rude bench cut out of the rock, and in one corner a low, narrow tunnel appeared. This, it was popularly said, ran to 'Quaker Hall's house. The entrance was barred by an iron grille, and all that could be seen, even with a light, was a sharply curved passage, the entrance being filled with sacks of potatoes. Of all the striking changes... the metamorphosis of Woden's Cave is one of the strangest. The site of the cave had become utterly forgotten by the time it came into the possession of Alderman Sir William Bailey, and it was then a coal yard. Ultimately the land was sold to the Corporation for the purpose of forming Emerald Street playground. On levelling the broken land, a great portion of the rock having been carried away, a great cavity was found under the surface, and this cavity, it is conjectured, was the once mysterious and romantic cave immortalized by Harrison Ainsworth. A more depressing spot, with its sordid surroundings, than this playground can hardly be imagined – that is, when its past beauty is recalled...'

The Ordsall that Harrison Ainsworth knew and roamed as a boy has disappeared but there is enough evidence to suggest that maybe, just maybe, there is more than a grain of truth in the story that Guy Fawkes and Robert Catesby met in the Star Chamber and discussed an impossible dream of blowing up the King and Parliament to free the Catholics from persecution. Only the Star Chamber knows what happened within its ancient walls and the secret is locked in the silence of that room.

96

From Ordsall to Salford Quays

1894 Salford Docks opened by Queen Victoria.

1896 Textiles, machinery, locomotives exported.

1905 King Edward VII and Queen Alexandra open No. 9 Dock.

1950s Docks working to capacity.

1970s Docks hit by industrial decline, changing trade patterns and containerisation.

1982 Docks closed; No. 2 grain elevator resists several attempts to blow it up.

1983 Salford City Council purchases Salford Quays and commissions architects.

1984 Production of development plan.

1985 Development plan published.

1980s Late in decade concept of a Salford Centre begins to emerge.

An aerial view of Salford and Ordsall, taken in 1932. (Manchester Archives and Local Studies Library, Central Library)

1991 Architects appointed to design this centre.

1996 Lottery funding obtained for Lowry Centre.

1997 Construction begins.

1998 National Waterways Festival.

2000 Lowry and Lowry Footbridge open 28 April.

2000 Official opening of Lowry by the Queen and Duke of Edinburgh on 12 October.

2001 Mixed retail, leisure, and residential development. Designer outlet opens in October.

2002 Imperial War Museum North opens on Trafford Wharf side in July.

2003 Digital World Centre opens.

2004 New apartments built.

The dock complex for the Manchester Ship Canal, which so much changed the face of Salford, closed in 1982 and a massive regeneration scheme for the area was put in place. It is now possible to take a walk through that piece of history starting from Ordsall Hall and ending at The Lowry on Salford Quays.

Leaving Ordsall Hall, cross Ordsall Lane and walk down to the former towpath of the ship canal through the Waters Edge Business Park and the Office Village. Passing Pomona (the end of the ship canal proper because the maximum draught was only 16ft) where shallower docks were built on the site of Pomona Pleasure Gardens, and the renowned Trafford Swing Bridge, turn downstream towards the Lowry. Upstream from Pomona on the Irwell lay the Tatton Egerton Mills and the Ordsall Rope Works.

The evocative names of the old quays along the way have been retained. Sandpiper's Quay stands close by Trafford Bridge. Clippers Quay is part of Salford Quays, but there are swans there now instead of sailing ships. Merchant's Quay is full of office blocks built of red brick in the style of the old shipping warehouses. St Francis Basin, between Clippers Quay and Merchant's Quay, houses the Lapinta, an old masted sailing ship, which today advertises *Lifestyle Furnishing*. There is also an elegant dockside restaurant, which charges what would have been more than a docker's weekly wage in the early days for a simple butty.

The towpath around St Francis Basin is overhung with young weeping willows, and former dockside cottages now have sun terraces and sell for very high prices. Round the next corner is Salford Quays and the Ontario Basin, which is dominated by a Holiday Inn and a watersports complex. At Welland Lock close by there is a bridge and at its head are two former dockside cranes, left in situ as a memorial to the former docklands.

The commemorative cranes and all that is left of the docks at Salford Quays.

As Ontario Basin rejoins the ship canal a small circular plaque proclaims:

> To let the sea flow in
> 34,000 hands
> moved 52 million tons
> of land

There is also a wall-side War Memorial to those who sailed from Salford in both World Wars and lost their lives. One in four British merchant seamen lost their lives at this time.

A centenary walkway was built in 1994 from Salford Quays to the Lowry Centre to commemorate 100 years since the opening of the Manchester Ship Canal. Large black bulwarks for tying up ships are still in place along the towpaths and walkway, and circular steel plaques along the way are full of philosophical quotes and stories of dockside life:

> We all remember
> something, someone
> and by recording the history
> of Salford
> these memories
> will never die

> In war or peace
> worse things always
> happen at sea

A very curious one conjures some wonderful word portraits:

> From Pearl White to Salome
> Shanghai Lil and Egg-on-Legs
> Handbag, Flipper, Cinderella.
> Tea-Pot Tommy, Rug-on-Head
> All these people we remember
> Madam Three Hairs
> All the rest

Salford Docks and the Manchester Ship Canal in 1891. (Manchester Archives and Local Studies Library, Central Library)

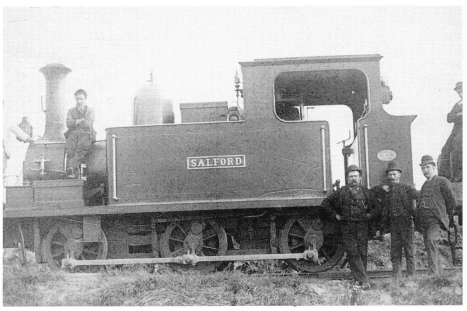

A Salford steam engine. (Manchester Archives and Local Studies Library, Central Library)

Unloading Australian wool in 1959. (Manchester Archives and Local Studies Library, Central Library)

Manchester Ship Canal

One of the biggest changes to Salford occurred with the building of the Manchester Ship Canal. The ship canal was built to link Manchester with the sea so that the city could trade internationally without incurring the prohibitive port charges levied by Liverpool and the high cost of

Construction of No. 9 Dock in 1903, before it was opened in 1905. (Manchester Archives and Local Studies Library, Central Library)

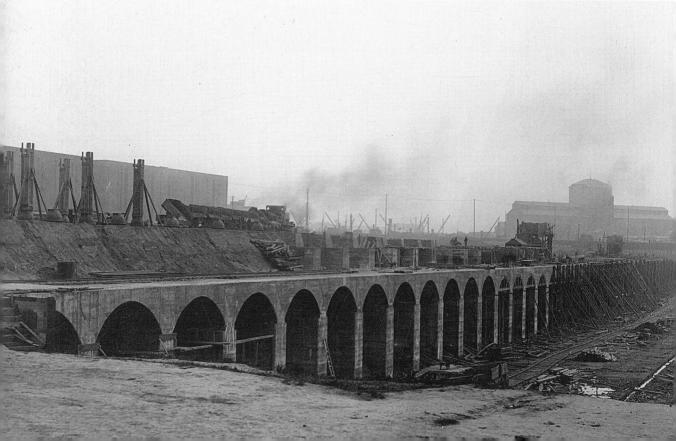

transporting freight by railway. Construction of the ship canal began in 1887 and was completed in 1894. It was a massive undertaking with over 17,000 people working on the project. Plant used included 75 steam excavators, 124 steam cranes and seven earth dredgers. The depth to which the canal was dug was the same as the Suez Canal. Locks were 65ft wide, as opposed to the normal 13ft width of canal locks. During excavations about a dozen simple canoes from the Norman period, which may have been used for carrying turf, peat, goods and people, were recovered from the Mersey and the Irwell. The ship canal was 35 miles long with triple entrance locks, and James Brindley achieved a unique feat of engineering by building the Barton Aqueduct to carry the Bridgewater Canal over the ship canal.

The Manchester Ship Canal was officially opened by Queen Victoria in 1894. A triumphal arch was built to celebrate the opening as a welcome to Salford and wishing success to the ship canal. There was an enormous complex of docks, most of which lay in Salford. Manchester and Salford Docks were one of the largest port authorities in the world and by 1914 had captured 5 percent of the UK import market and 4.4 percent of the domestic exports market. Cotton, wool, grain, steam locomotives and

Images of the Salford Docks from 1894, showing a cotton steamer and the warehouse. (Manchester Archives and Local Studies Library, Central Library)

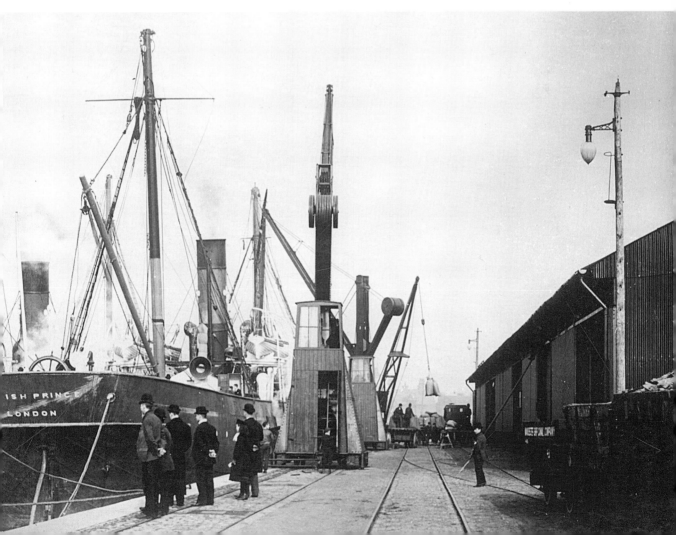

Another two
images of the
Salford Docks
from 1894.
(Manchester
Archives and
Local Studies
Library, Central
Library)

textile machinery, were just some of the commodities handled. No. 9 Dock, the largest of the docks, was opened in 1905 by King Edward VII and Queen Alexandra.

A variety of commodities passed through the docks during the post-cotton boom years; both import and export goods. Some cotton, of course, was still exported until the 1960s but the range of other goods included cattle and sheep (frozen and live), coal, carbon, lamp black, bananas, coconuts, animal hides, horns and bones, barrage balloons, trains, boats, planes, cars, wool, linen and the packed sections of Agecroft Hall on their way to Virginia.

The ship canal's peak years were the 1950s, but changes were coming. The cotton trade had been declining since the early 1920s. Changes in local manufacturing industries led to shifting trading patterns and competition on North Atlantic shipping routes, plus various mergers and take-over bids during the 1970s combined to cause a serious decline in

River Irwell, Salford Bank. (Manchester Archives and Local Studies Library, Central Library)

cargo handling by the docks. In addition, new ocean going container ships and tankers had become too large for the docks to handle. There was also not much traffic sailing the full 36 miles of the ship canal and it was possible to sail from Salford to Manchester along the navigable sections of the Mersey and the Irwell. It was considered closing the upper reaches of the ship canal during the 1980s and the docks finally closed in 1982.

Salford Quays

Green's Map of 1794 shows the original Salford Quay on the north bank of the Irwell between Blackfriar's Bridge and New Bridge, close to the New Bailey Prison and the lying-in hospital and not far south of St Mary's

*The New Bailey Prison and the Lying-in Hospital, 1804.
(Manchester Archives and Local Studies Library, Central Library)*

*Looking towards the New Bailey Prison from the old Salford 'key', 1829.
(Manchester Archives and Local Studies Library, Central Library)*

Premier Lodge on the site of the former lying-in Hospital.

Church and St Mary's Parsonage on the Manchester side. This was the limit of the river navigation in 1794. Salford Key, as it was termed, was served by 'sailing flats', which had a shallow draught and could work both on the rivers and on the Mersey estuary. In the 1740s about 20 'flats' were regularly working from Liverpool to Salford Quay. The Salford Key Company, river navigation carriers, rivalled the Duke of Bridgewater's

Salford Docks jetty in 1891, showing Dock Nos. 1 and 2. (Manchester Archives and Local Studies Library, Central Library)

canal enterprise so he purchased shares on a gradual basis, and by 1779 he owned the Salford Key Company completely. Quay Street in Salford led from Salford Quay and the present Blackfriar's Street was then (1794) named Water Street.

New Buildings at Salford Quays as part of the regeneration project that has taken place there.

Modern blocks of flats in Salford, 2004.

All that remains of the docks at Salford Quays, 2004.

Left: *New offices near to the Lowry at Salford Quays.*

Right: *The Eagle Totem Pole, outside Salford Customs and Excise.*

The surviving Dock Office in Salford.

Docks Nos.1–4 were further up the river at Pomona, and Trafford Swing Bridge gave ships access to these docks. Salford Quays were a venture initiated on the ship canal by Dukinfield engineering firm owner Daniel Adamson in 1882, which was opened for traffic by Queen Victoria on 1 January 1894. Adamson did not live to see this, having died in 1890, aged 71. The water basins of Docks 8, 7 and 6 were named Ontario, Huron and Erie to commemorate Canadian trading links.

Today the Quays have become home to office blocks and the service industries. Across the road from Salford Quays stands Ontario House, home to the Department of Employment. Anchorage Quay lies behind Merchant's Quay near the dock's offices, which still survive, and has modern office blocks built of red brick in 19th-century warehouse-style. Furness House (formerly the offices of Manchester Liners who transferred to Ellesmere Port in 1983) at the rear of Anchorage Quay is, perhaps appropriately, now home to HM Customs and Excise and is fronted, again perhaps appropriately, by what appears to be an 'eagle totem pole'. Merchant's Quay also has office blocks of a similar nature to Anchorage Quay.

The Lowry shopping centre.

The Lowry

The Lowry is part of the docks regeneration scheme and is built on a tongue of land between the sites of the former No. 8 Dock, to the east, and No. 9 Dock, to the west. The project takes its name from one of Salford's most famous sons, the internationally renowned painter L.S. Lowry (see Pendlebury). The Lowry complex includes the Lyric Theatre and the Quays Theatre, which between them can seat over 2,000 people; art galleries, which display the collected work of L.S. Lowry; bars, cafes, shops, information centres and Artworks (a creative community project); the Digital World Centre; a unique lifting footbridge over the ship canal and the Imperial War Museum. At the head of this complex and to the west are the commercial developments of Anchorage and Harbour City.

The basins were stocked with 12,000 coarse fish to attract anglers. A multiplex cinema, a watersports centre and upmarket housing formed the

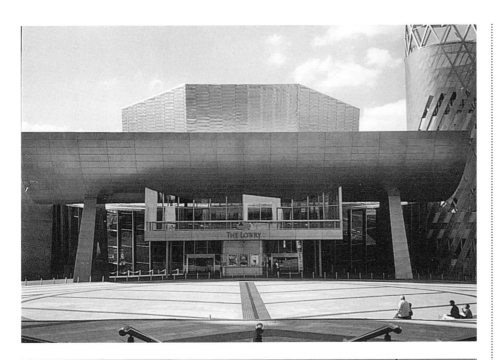

The Lowry theatres and art gallery.

Metrolink at Harbour City, The Lowry, in Salford.

World Digital Centre at Salford Quays, 2004.

The Imperial War
Museum,
offering an
unusual and
unique insight
into the meaning
of war.

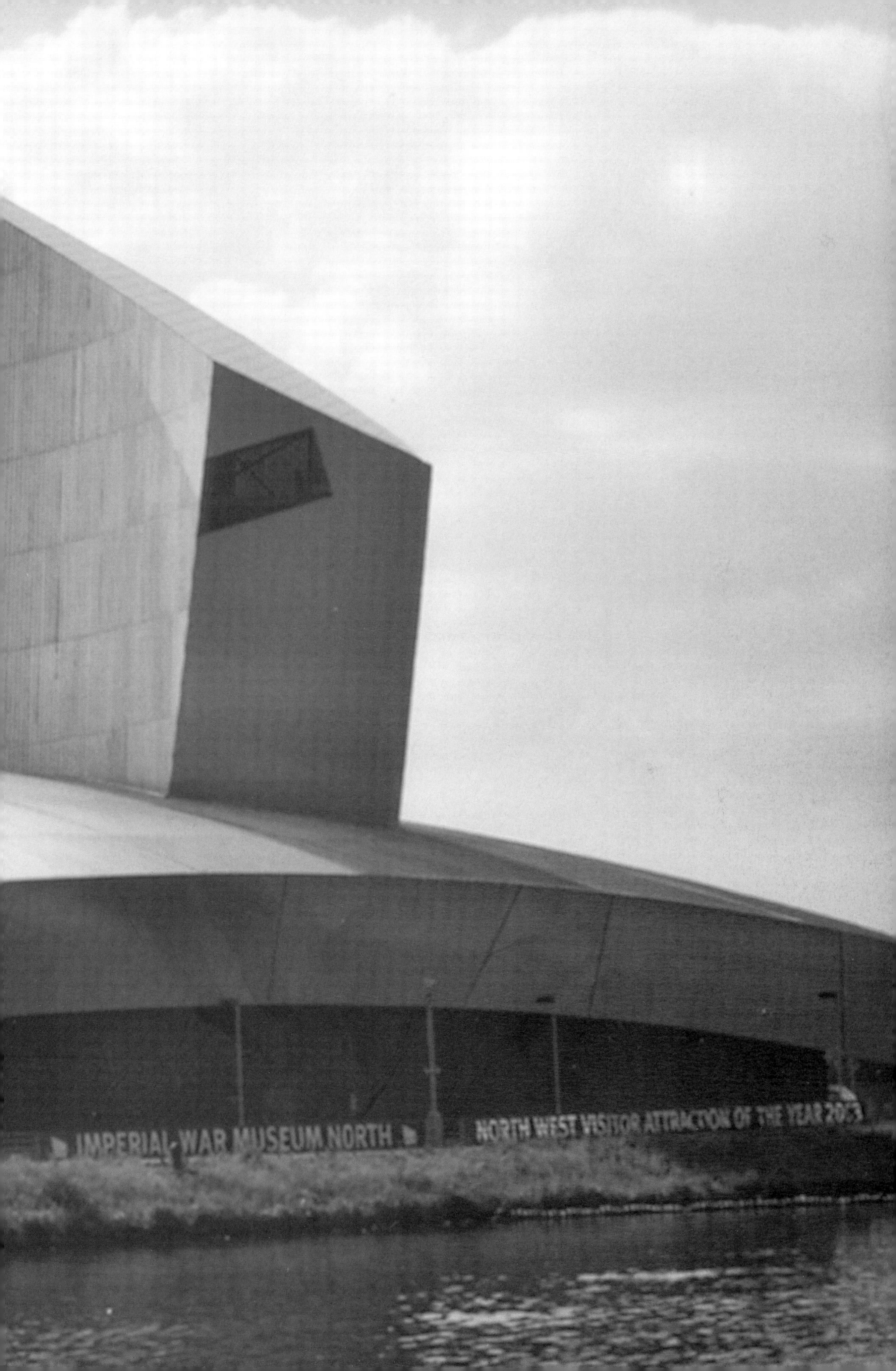
IMPERIAL WAR MUSEUM NORTH
NORTH WEST VISITOR ATTRACTION OF THE YEAR

Modern apartments at Harbour City.

first elements of regeneration and attracting investment and people to the area. An extensive network of footpaths was landscaped. The whole project has been an innovative way of '...replacing an industrial ghost town with artistic, creative and vibrant ventures so that leisure industry not heavy industry is now the thing...'.

Opposite page:
The moving suspension bridge at The Lowry.

Districts of Salford

Broughton

Broughton was popular in early times for its forests of game and the fish-stocked River Irwell, which ran through the lower part of the area. Traces of a Roman villa have been discovered in Albert Park and a number of Roman coins have been found in Broughton. However, generally, little is known of its history until the 19th century. Broughton lay in Manchester ecclesiastical parish but within Salford Poor Law Union until 1844 when part of it was included in Salford Borough, the remainder being transferred in 1853. Broughton Local Board of Health was established in 1851. There is a description of Broughton given in 1841 by Edwin Butterworth:

The River Irwell and Broughton Bridge millscape, c.1895. (Salford Local Studies Library)

Broughton, a township in the parish of Manchester, and parliamentary borough of Salford. Number of acres 1,338: 1 miles N.N.W. of Manchester. There are traces of a small Roman fortress. Here is a new church, St. John the Evangelist's, built 1836-7, cost £6,000. The Wesleyans have a chapel. The township is lighted and watched by direction of a rate-payers' committee. There are silk and flax manufactories: and numerous rural villas. In 1801 the population was 866; 1811, 825; 1821, 880; 1831, 1,589. In 1835 the day schools were 8, Sunday 1, scholars 467. In Higher Broughton are the Zoological Gardens, upwards of 15 acres in extent, opened 1838. On Kersall-moor Manchester races take place. The value of property in 1815 was £5,044;

1829, £14,528. The boulder stones near Kersall are remarkable.
(A Statistical Sketch of the County Palatine of Lancaster, Edwin Butterworth, 1841.)

Differentiation between Broughton, Higher Broughton and Lower Broughton followed and is reflected in the list of churches for the area:

Camp Street/Great Clowes Street Primitive Methodist, Broughton
Bury New Road Congregational, Broughton
Salem Methodist, Broughton (Bury New Road)
Great Cheetham Street West Wesleyan Methodist, Higher Broughton
St Clements, Lower Broughton (Broughton lane)
The Ascension, Lower Broughton (Clarence Street)
Alexandra Gardens Methodist, Broughton
St Boniface, Lower Broughton (St Boniface Road)
Great Clowes Street Union Baptist, Lower Broughton
Sussex Street Wesleyan Methodist, Lower Broughton
Salem Methodist, Higher Broughton (Wellington Street)
St James, Higher Broughton (Great Cheetham Street East)
St John the Evangelist, Higher Broughton (Murray Street)
St Thomas of Canterbury, Higher Broughton (Great Cheetham Street East)

Broughton Hall was the home of the Earls of Derby and of the Clowes family. The Clowes family inherited the hall in 1772 from the Chetham family. It was demolished in 1913 but the site and grounds were opened as Clowes Park in 1929 by Salford Corporation. There were woodlands

St John's Church in Broughton, 1850. (Manchester Archives and Local Studies Library, Central Library)

around Broughton but timber was commercially exploited in the 19th century, although as late as 1936 it was still possible to gather armfuls of bluebells in the Broughton woodlands in springtime.

Broughton Zoological Gardens stood at the junction of Bury New Road and Northumberland Street in Higher Broughton for four years

An Edwardian wedding in Broughton in 1906. (Manchester Archives and Local Studies Library, Central Library)

Broughton Park Church in 1902. (Manchester Archives and Local Studies Library, Central Library)

from 1838–42. Albert Park opened in 1877 though its two-acre lake was drained and infilled during the 1940s. Albert Park Library opened in 1890, but it was bombed and burned out in December 1940. The library was later rebuilt on Great Clowes Street. Great Clowes Street, in the Cliff area of Higher Broughton, collapsed in July 1927 after a storm because of undercutting by the River Irwell. Lower Broughton was badly flooded in September 1946. Water was 4ft deep in Broughton Lane and 5,000 people were made homeless.

Broughton Spout, now in the Cliff area of Broughton, was the cottage home of William Crabtree (1610–44), an early astronomer who worked on sunspots, planetary motions and collaborated with Jeremiah Horrocks in recording the Transit of Venus in November 1639 (see also William Crabtree). The cottages were demolished in 1810 but a plaque marks the spot where they were believed to have stood.

The Manchester Carriage Company Ltd had a depot at the corner of Knoll Street and Bury New Road where stabling and maintenance facilities were provided for horse-drawn trams between 1877–1901, until the trams were electrified. Stotts' Motors used the building from the 1920s–70s. In July 1920 Salford's first motor bus ran from Great

CWS timber and wheelwrights in 1925. (Manchester Archives and Local Studies Library, Central Library)

Cheetham Street in Broughton to Pendleton. The bus had solid tyres and could carry 45 passengers.

Broughton Baths on Great Clowes Street (between Muriel Street and Lucy Street) opened in 1890, having been built at some considerable cost. There were first and second class pools, slipper and vapour baths. They were closed in 1935. Broughton Rangers were a well-known rugby team who played on Wheater's Field and then, from 1913, at The Cliff. They disbanded in 1956.

The Devonshire Cinema stood on Devonshire Street and opened on 18 January 1913. Later it became both a theatre and a cinema, but by 1963 it was being used as a tombola club and in the 1970s the building was demolished. The Calderwood Day Centre now stands on the site. Two pubs, called The Beehive and Poet's Corner, stood on Lower Broughton Road, but in 1976 intervening shops were demolished and the building became one pub named Poets Corner; an echo of the famous Poet's Corner pub (The Rising Sun) on Long Millgate in Manchester.

Today the population of Broughton is around 2,500 and the main industries are retail and trade motor mechanics and health and social service work.

Kersal

The name Kersal originated as 'Keres-hel, derived from 'carr', meaning a wood situated on boggy grassland, and 'hale', from the Anglo-Saxon Mercian 'healh', which means a piece of land at the bend of a river. Neolithic tools have been discovered on Kersal Moor and the area has been settled for some three to four thousand years. According to one historical writer, in 1907, '...native forest tracks along the foot of Strangeways, up Kersal, originated the Roman gravel high road in that part...', but the earliest written record of Kersal occurs in the reign of Stephen (1142), when the tiny hamlet was granted to the Cluniac Order of the Holy Trinity Priory, near Lenton in Nottinghamshire, by Randolph Gernons, Earl of Chester, so that '...a place could be built for the service of God...' Kersal Cell was the small monastic cell built for this purpose by the Benedictine monks, near the ford at Agecroft. It was dedicated to St Leonard. Not richly endowed, it was probably a single-storey 'crucked' building, originally intended for just one monk, hence the name cell. The monks were also given permission to '...enlarge to themselves the assarts [clearings made by chopping down trees in the woodlands] and the fisheries and all other things whatsoever which they can enlarge or give ease to themselves...' Hugh de Buron became the first inhabitant of the cell. He was a hermit monk and '...he could pace the oak woods which lay in front [of the cell]... there were fine pastures and meadows in the

Kersal Cell in the 1920's. (Manchester Archives and Local Studies Library, Central Library)

rich alluvial land for the milk kine [domesticated cattle] and the goats and the lambs, and situations for apiaries in the forest for the wax candles of the altar...the river abounded then in trout, grayling, perch, carp, dace, bream, and eels...'

The north wing is older and built from stone used for the monastic buildings. An oak door in the west wall led to the chapel and upper floor with its Priest's Room and also various 'priest hidey-holes'. The Priest's Room occupied the southern end above the Sun Dial Room.

Henry II reaffirmed the grant for Kersal Cell in 1182. The monks were permitted to extend the assarts for which a tax was usually payable to the

Kersal Cell, on 12 April 1925. (Salford Local Studies Library)

King, though in 1199 King John gave Jornechio de Hulton the village of Pendleton in exchange for 'Kereshall Wood', which the king no doubt wanted for hunting. Between 1298 and 1405 the cell was recorded as having one prior and one monk in residence at a time. Gradually more monks joined them and they built a mill to grind their corn on the Mill Brook and planted orchards at the back of the cell. They had a kiln for pottery making, a grange, crofts and arable fields, and generally the monastic community was self-supporting and viable. Kersal Cell fell victim to the Dissolution of the Monasteries by Henry VIII in 1536, and it was then sold, with Kersal Manor, in 1540, to Baldwin Willoughby.

The cell was enlarged and eventually acquired by the Byrom family in 1613. It remained within their family until 1870 when it became a girl's boarding school for about 30 years before reverting to a private house. In 1994 a modern housing estate was built around the cell. Structural surveys of Kersal Cell in 1946 revealed the existence of tunnels, which had been built in the mid-18th century and led to the River Irwell and Manchester Cathedral. Legend has it that John Byrom was a secret Jacobite and used the tunnels to attend clandestine meetings and to reach his house in Manchester. Certainly, in 1745, he had watched Bonnie Prince Charlie's triumphant entrance into Manchester from his house in the Shambles. John Byrom, born in 1692, invented a system of phonetic shorthand, which was a forerunner to the better known Pitman's shorthand. He was also an accomplished poet and linguist and he wrote the hymn *Christians Awake*, which he is said to have sung to his wife, Dorothy, on the snowy Christmas morning of 1751.

Overlooking Kersal Vale, the astronomer William Crabtree lived in a house quaintly named Broughton Spout. Crabtree, born in 1610, was friendly with teacher and astronomer Jeremiah Horrocks and William Gascoigne. The three of them formed various theories on planetary orbits and in 1639 Jeremiah Horrocks was the first to discover the Transit of

Venus, which takes place only every 120 years (see section on William Crabtree).

In 1927 F.A. Bruton wrote that '...Salford came to Manchester for education while Manchester came to Salford for her amusements...'

Since the 1600s racing had been held on 'Carsalle Moor', as it was then called. In 1687 a 'twenty pound plate' was run on the Clowes Estate up on Kersal Moor. Dr John Byrom, who lived at Kersal Cell, disapproved of gambling and protested against the Races in 1733 by writing a strongly worded pamphlet with the punchy title of: 'A Serious Dissuasive from an Intended Subscription for continuing the Races upon Kersal Moor'. His arguments were based on moral and religious grounds and forcibly put '...to believe like a Christian and to act like a Pagan is as monstrous in the moral world as anything that was ever produced in the material world...' He did not succeed, although racing was suspended from 1745–60. This, however, might have had more to do with the political situation than Dr Byrom's moral stance. 1745 was the year in which Bonnie Prince Charlie marched south to claim the English crown, and the fact that he got as far as Derby with little resistance left the authorities and the king, George II, feeling distinctly jittery. By 1760 the situation was far more stable and a new king, George III, had ascended the throne.

In 1763 smiles were raised when the last horse in a particular race turned out to be called Creeping Jane '...a pretty lady who never minded being left behind...' By 1772 Whitsuntide had been recognised as Race Week, instead of sometime in August, September or October. A Grandstand was built in 1777 and, three years afterwards, the Ladies

Stand opened with '...tea, coffee and chocolate to be provided...by Elizabeth Raffald...' an excellent cook and housekeeper who wrote a book of 18th-century recipes, which is still available.

During the 1730s the notorious highwayman Dick Turpin was a regular attender at the Races. Turpin spent the last few years of his life at Brough in Yorkshire, always managing to keep just one step ahead of the law. He was fond of drinking, gambling and women, and he attended the Races with his married girlfriend, who disguised herself as a boy to avoid recognition. The Manchester newspapers reported his sheer nerve in attending such an event so openly and so too did the London morning newspapers. Despite this, Turpin's luck held and he indulged his passion for racing freely. He was only captured when he annoyed a neighbour in Yorkshire by shooting his squawking cockerel.

Manchester Golf Club opened the second golf course in England and five holes of that course lay on Kersal Moor Racecourse from 1687 until the Racecourse closed in 1846. The Races had continued to grow in size and popularity so that eventually another home had to be found for them. At first, Fairfield in Manchester was designated and a large railway station with several platforms was built to accommodate trains bringing people to the Races. However, it was decided to keep the Races in Salford, and Fairfield was left with a huge empty ghost station. Castle Irwell was the site chosen, and in 1847 the Races moved there.

Castle Irwell has been somewhat unkindly described as an '...unsightly, unsanitary and unsafe castellated brick house...' Whatever the truth, it was demolished in 1900 to make way for a new racecourse, which opened in 1902. The first ever Irish Sweepstake was run on this racecourse in 1930 and, due to World War Two, it was decided to run the St Ledger there as well, in 1941. A 'record race' took place on 12 November 1959 when 171 horses entered for a six race card. The last racing meeting held on the Castle Irwell Racecourse was in November 1963. In 1967 the site was purchased by Salford University for building student accommodation.

Castle Irwell, c.1870, demolished to make way for race course facilities. (Salford Local Studies Library)

Castle Irwell, photographed in 1870. (Manchester Archives and Local Studies Library, Central Library)

One of the strangest sights seen on Kersal Moor has to have been in 1887 when Bill Cody, better known as Buffalo Bill, and the Red Indian Chief Sitting Bull performed a Wild West Show with a party of Indian chiefs and braves, who had accompanied them on a visit to England. There is an old photograph in Manchester Central Library archives of Buffalo Bill and Chief Sitting Bull taken on a tram, probably at Belle Vue where they also performed, together with the rest of the chiefs and braves in full Red Indian war costume and feathered headdresses, looking for all the world as though they were on a day trip to Blackpool.

Before the Industrial Revolution the main livelihoods in Kersal were farming, a cottage textile industry, rope making and fishing. Until the 18th century the River Irwell was well stocked with fish, including salmon, and fishing was an important local industry. Kersal Vale Bleachworks, which stood on the site of the former Corn Mill, was just one of the many local businesses whose effluent polluted streams and rivers, killing the fish and any other underwater creatures unlucky enough to live there. After the coming of the mills and manufactories, with the attendant population explosion as workers moved into the area looking for jobs, commercial premises and cramped rows of terraced cottages swallowed up much of the surrounding countryside. Churches and schools followed. St Paul's Church was built in 1851 and consecrated in

1852. It had an unusual double spire '...like a mother and child...' St Aidan's on Littleton Road was a mission building dedicated in 1911. St Paul's Church of England Primary School was built in 1863 on Kersal Moor, although it was rebuilt in 1976 on a new site in nearby Neville Road. Lower Kersal Junior and Infant School was not opened until the 1930s. It was built around three sides of a courtyard garden and the fourth side was enclosed in 1958.

During the 1920s the well-known soap manufacturer, Alexander Cussons, transferred his soap works from Swinton to Kersal. Cussons and Sons 'manufacturing chemists and dry salters', as they were known, moved to a site by Singleton Brook and occupied the old Kersal Vale Bleachworks. Production of toilet preparations gradually took over as the main part of their business, and in 1938 Imperial Leather soap was introduced. It was inspired by the 'Eau de Cologne Imperiale Russe',

St Paul's Church, Kersal Moor, in 1851, before it was consecrated the following year. (Manchester Archives and Local Studies Library, Central Library)

which was created for the Russian Court in 1917, shortly before the overthrow of the Tsar. During the latter half of the 20th century Cussons moved the manufacturing side of the business to Nottingham; but in 2005 the wheel turned full circle and Cussons have announced the closure of their Nottingham works and the transfer of their manufacturing business to Thailand and Indonesia. Now the soap that began life in Salford will be imported from Asia for its English customers.

Worsley

1086	Mentioned in Domesday Book.
1195	Hugh Poutrell gives Richard de Workesley the manors of Worsley and Hulton for services rendered.
1233	Ellenbrook Chapel built.
1276	Worsley Old Hall already built.
1385	Male line of Worsley family dies out and Worsley passes, through marriage, to the Massey family.
1480	Worsley passes to the Brereton family.
1575	Richard Brereton Junior dies.
1598	Richard Brereton Senior, who had married Dorothy Egerton, dies and Worsley passes to her half brother, Sir Thomas Egerton.
1745	1st Duke of Bridgewater dies.
1748	2nd Duke of Bridgewater dies and title passes to his younger brother.
1748	Francis Egerton, 3rd Duke of Bridgewater, inherits Worsley.
1759	Duke of Bridgewater's canal built from Worsley to Manchester by James Brindley.
1803	The 3rd Duke of Bridgewater dies unmarried and without issue. Worsley passes to his great-nephew, Francis Leveson-Gower, who changes his name to Egerton.
1846	Francis Egerton (nee Leveson-Gower) is created Earl of Ellesmere.
1846	Building of Worsley New Hall by Earl of Ellesmere commences.
1869	Walkden Monument to Harriet, Countess of Ellesmere and widow of Francis Egerton (nee Leveson-Gower).
1894	Worlsey Urban District Council formed.
1903	Bridgewater Trustees cease administration of Worsley.
1918	Industries diversify as coal and cotton industries begin to decline.
1933	District Councils of Worsley and Little Hulton amalgamate.
1945	Worsley becomes Salford 'overspill dormitory'.
1949	Worsley New Hall demolished.
1974	Worsley becomes a part of the new City of Salford.

Opposite: St Paul's Church in 1939. (Manchester Archives and Local Studies Library, Central Library)

Two Roman roads are said to have passed through Worsley: one going from Manchester to Wigan; the other passing through Walkden and Little Hulton along the line of the present A6. In 1947 a hoard of 540 Roman coins was discovered in a stone quarry in neighbouring Boothstown. The coins are said to have come from Gaul and are dated between AD 251 and AD 275. Worsley may derive from 'workes', Old English for work, and 'ley', meaning clearing, indicating that the area was first settled in its present form in Saxon times. After the Norman Conquest Worsley lay in the manor of Barton. In the Domesday Book of 1086 the manor included part of Swinton and Pendlebury, part of Kearsley and Chat Moss as far as Cadishead.

The first official mentions come later. Hugh Poultrell gave the manors of Worsley and Hulton to '...Richard, son of Elias de Workesley, for his homage and service...' in 1195, and in 1203 Richard de Worsley was recorded as the owner of 20 acres of Worsley Wood. In 1305 there is mention of a water mill and, by 1376, a moated manor house with messauges (barns, yards and outbuildings). This would have been Worsley Old Hall.

There was also a Peel, which is a fortified tower. Licences were granted by the clerks at Eccles for a chapel at Ellenbrook in 1220–1233; and in 1276 a licence was granted for a free chantry in the chapel. Ellenbrook Chapel was initially built in the form of a cross, but was rebuilt in 1725 as a single hall. The Court Leet (a kind of magistrates court) met regularly from 1195 onwards and continued to do so until 1856. During the 18th century the court met in the Grapes Inn, which stood on the site of the roundabout near the present Courthouse, built in 1849.

Worsley Estate had a complicated history and passed through marriage to several families including the Masseys, the Breretons and the Egertons. A rough summary shows the ownership thus:

    14th century Worsleys
    15th century Masseys and Stanleys
    16th century Breretons
    17th century Egertons
    18th century Egertons

All of them lived in Worsley Old Hall, which was described as still moated during the reign of Henry VI (1422–61). The last of the Breretons were Richard and Dorothy (née Egerton). Dorothy Egerton endowed a charity that is still distributed in Worsley and Hulton. Their only son, Richard, died when he was a small child and with him died the family line. When Richard Senior died he left Worsley Old Hall to Thomas Egerton, Dorothy's half brother, from whom the Dukes of Bridgewater were directly descended. As a 19th-century writer was to observe '...the passing of that little life set gigantic forces in motion two hundred years later...'

Sir Thomas Egerton, Lord High Chancellor of England and owner of Worsley Old Hall, was created Viscount Brackley in 1616. His son, John, the 1st Earl of Bridgewater, succeeded to the Worsley estate in 1639. The 4th Earl of Bridgewater (1701–1745) was made the 1st Duke of Bridgewater. The 2nd Duke of Bridgewater (1745–1748) died of smallpox at Eton. His younger brother, Francis, became the 3rd Duke of Bridgewater (1748–1803), and he was responsible for developing the Worsley coal mines and the building of the Bridgewater Canal. Francis died unmarried and without issue and the Dukedom lapsed. He built the Brick Hall during the 1760s as a house for his agent, John Gilbert.

Francis, 3rd Duke of Bridgewater, was a pioneer of the canal system of transport in Northern England along the model of Dutch 'treckschuyts', of which a contemporary wrote: '...to persons not in a hurry, afford a very pleasant transit at a reasonable rate...' The Duke was not particularly concerned about people, but he was concerned about getting coal from his 'extensive collieries' in Worsley to the heart of Manchester. In 1760 there were no railways and the roads were poor and often impassable. The river was not navigable in places either so the Duke and his engineer, James Brindley (who also spent some time living at Brick Hall), devised a plan for a navigable waterway that would transport coal directly from the mines to Manchester quickly and cheaply. James Brindley preferred his waterways to be level, and he did not approve of the numerous locks and weirs of the Irwell and Mersey River navigation because he felt that they slowed traffic down as well as wasting time and effort.

'*...it was the principle of Mr Brindley to keep his canals as much of a level as possible; it became necessary, therefore, to carry them over roads and streams upon arches, and to fill up valleys by artificial mounds, as well as to cut down and bore through hills...*'

In 1758–59 the Duke obtained the necessary Acts of Parliament, which would allow him to build a canal from Worsley to Salford and also to Hollin Ferry on the Mersey and to carry his canal from Worsley across the River Irwell to Manchester through Stretford. He and Brindley had come up with the ingenious idea of a '...subterranean navigation...of about 40 miles in extent...all [of] which is continuous and on a level with the coal, which goes to the great depot of merchandise and [to] the docks at Runcorn...'

A writer of the 1830s describes the beginning of this unique project: '*...at its upper extremity in Worsley the canal forms a large basin, and an entrance is made in a hill by an arched passage...which...penetrates nearly three quarters of a mile before it reaches the first coal works. It* *then divides into two channels, diverging to the right and left, which have been continued in various branches...perpendicular air holes are cut at certain distances through to solid rock...*' When the canal finally emerged into daylight it crossed the River Irwell via an aqueduct at Barton Bridge, the first of its kind seen in England, and was '*...thence conveyed without locks by a circuitous tract of nine miles to Castlefield...over the swampy ground of Trafford Moss, a labour infinitely exceeding that of constructing the aqueduct...*'

The canal arch into the rock at the Delph was about 6ft high and 5ft wide. Underground, the waterways were on four levels. The main one was 9ft high by 9ft wide and 4ft deep. Levels two and three were respectively 168ft and 249ft below the main line and the fourth and deepest level was 420ft below the main line, really quite deep. The system provided canal access to all the coal workings.

There had been coal mining in Worsley from around 1376. Originally it was open cast mining, but by the early 17th century 'bell pits and day eye holes' were used to reach coal on Big and Little Lady Hills on the Worsley demesne, to the east of Worsley Old Hall. There were also mine shafts at Abbots Fold, Ellenbrook, Edge Fold, Lumber Lane, Walkden Road (then known as Shaving Lane) and Standish Street, as well as on Walkden Moor and at Wood Pit in Worsley Woods.

The underground canal, known as the 'Navigable Level', started at the Delph in Worsley and ran north-west under Walkden and Little Hulton to Dixon Green. Work began in 1759, with teams of miners cutting the rock by hand with pick, shovel and hammer. There were twin tunnels from Worsley Delph to Watersmeet. When this part of the project was complete, there were four levels of canals with numerous side branches, giving a total of 52 miles of underground waterways. The tunnels were narrow and often not very high. They were lined with bricks fired in the Duke's own kilns. There were no towpaths and the narrow boats or barges, which could carry seven or eight tons each, were either towed by handrails on each side or worked by the feet. The bargee would lie on his back in the boat and work his feet along the tunnel roof. It was dark and claustrophobic but challenging and exciting; '*...an intricately immaculate feat of engineering...*' Visitors came from near and far to witness this unique and innovative system of underground waterways. Many were local; several were foreign; a few were famous and included King Christian VII of Denmark (who also brought 50 of his courtiers with him) in 1768; the Russian Princess Czartoriski, Duchess of Oldenburg in 1778; Archdukes John and Lewis of Austria with a team of scientific advisers in 1815 and Grand Duke Nicholas, later Czar of Russia, in 1817.

A Manchester Scientific Students' Report of 1881 noted, after a tour of the underground canals, that '...the bricks today...many are as good and new as in the 1760s... the roof of the tunnel is frescoed by nature's own pencil. Fast bedded in the rocks are fossil ferns, the fronds and stems most exquisitely traced...' There was the ever-present problem of silting in the canals, but the underground system was used for transporting coal until 1887. Afterwards it served as a drainage mechanism for local coal pits, finally becoming redundant when the last pit closed in 1968.

In 1761 the Runcorn Branch Canal was built from the Bridgewater Canal, which '...branching...at the distance of three miles from Manchester, passes over the low grounds in the township of Stretford, upon a vast mound of earth of great length and of wonderful construction; it leaves the county of Lancaster by an aqueduct bridge across the Mersey...then traverses Cheshire till it falls into the Mersey at Runcorn Gap...by a series of locks; having thus no impediment...the voyage is much speedier...than that of the Irwell and Mersey Navigation with its numerous locks and weirs...' A branch from the Bridgewater Canal at Worsley to Leigh was begun in 1795, which was subsequently extended to Wigan by the Leeds and Liverpool Canal Company.

The Duke's Tunnel, as it became known, was built in 1787: an underground canal designed to carry coals from his Bridgewater Canal at Castlefield, across the City of Manchester, to a coal wharf close to where Piccadilly railway station now stands and the Piccadilly Basin where the Rochdale and Ashton Canals met. The canal is now 'silted up and deeply buried'; the only visible evidence of its existence is the top of a curved archway a few inches above the level of the water at a curve in the Medlock where it passes between the back of Asia House and the rear of Charles Street car park

During the first part of the 18th century the main industries in Worsley were rural, including farming (mostly growing of oats and wheat) and fustian weaving, which was a cottage industry, but there was also a black lead factory, the lead being used for pencils and preservation of ironwork (black leading fire grates etc.). Woodlands were '...abundantly stocked with game...' Surrounding hamlets regarded as a part of Worsley in 1830 included Boothstown, Ellenbrook, Little Houghton, New Town, Shaving Lane, Swinton and Walkden Moor, beneath which lay a number of valuable coal mines. The latter part of the century saw an increase in coal mining (there was Edge Fold Colliery on Walkden Road and Mangalls Colliery on Wilfred Road – the British Legion Club now stands on the site of the latter), brick manufacture in kilns and the emergence of the canal transport system, thanks to the efforts of the 3rd Duke of Bridgewater.

In 1853 Worsley was described as:

'...one of the prettiest villages of which our island can boast... [on]the

*Home kiln at
Worsley, near
the Delph, in
1807. (Salford
Local Studies
Library)*

*road skirting the banks of the canal... are tastefully laid out pleasure
gardens... passing onwards, the eye is strikingly impressed with the
extreme air of cleanliness, comfort and picturesque beauty which pervades
the entire village, from the humble cottage to the stately mansion; houses
with their stuccoed and lime washed walls glistening in the sun amidst
blooming gardens...gracefully relieved by the verdant foliage of
neighbouring trees...and the elegant church ...the elegant bridge over the
canal, and the romantic aspect of the rock , at whose base... [are] vast
subterranean canals... form one of the most pleasing localities...'*

The road through Worsley became a toll road from 1753 until 1870.
The Toll House stood at the Toll Barm, which was situated at the junction
of Broad Oak Road and Worsley Road. The London and North Western
railway (LNWR) line reached Worsley and Walkden in 1864 and 1875
respectively and each had their own station. Walkden also had a station,
which opened in 1888, on Shaving Lane (now Walkden Road) for the
Lancashire and Yorkshire railway. This station is still open but the
LNWR station at Walkden closed in 1954. Worsley escaped the excesses
of the millscapes because it lay too far out and the population in 1871
was just 15,387, a fraction of Manchester suburbs such as Ancoats or
Chorlton-on-Medlock. However, Worsley had begun to grow in size. St
Mark's Church was built in 1846. It had a '...very handsome lofty spire,
beautifully proportioned, and three bells...' and could seat 800 people.
There was also a Wesleyan Chapel. There were National Schools for both
boys and girls and a Sunday School; Worsley Technical School; a
subscription reading room and a library and, by 1873, a new Town Hall.
In 1868 the Bridgewater Trustee offices were built in Walkden, a district
of Worsley. The works yard for the mines, canals, and estate was
demolished in 1905 (two years after the Trustees ceased administration of

Worsley) and the area is now covered by The Green. Close by stood a curiously named 18th-century inn known as The Swan with Two Nicks. It was rebuilt in 1898 and renamed in 1900 as the Stocks Hotel (on account of it having stood near the stocks), becoming a terminus for the Walkden-Farnworth horse bus service.

Worsley lay in Barton upon Irwell Poor Law Union and Eccles ecclesiastical parish, and from 1867 part of the town was included under Swinton Local Board of Health (Swinton and Pendlebury Board of health from 1869). In 1892 a fraction of Worsley was given to Eccles Borough and two years later the part that had been included under Swinton Local Board of Health became Swinton township and, therefore, part of Swinton and Pendlebury Urban District Council. What remained became Worsley Urban District in 1894. The new Council had its first offices in the former railway refreshment rooms at Walkden. To this was added, in 1921, the 21 acres said to form Barton upon Irwell civil parish. In 1933 Little Hulton Urban District was added to Worsley Urban District; part of Worsley Urban District was added to Eccles (and later in 1955 another small part was given to Swinton and Pendlebury Council) and areas of land were exchanged with Irlam Urban District. Some things don't change and it would seem that this includes the complexities of local government boundaries. Finally, in 1974, Worsley became part of Salford Metropolitan District, the new City of Salford (GMRCO).

One of the more unusual inhabitants of Worsley was Polly the Pig. Polly gave birth to 200 piglets during her life time and it was perhaps this that drove her to drink. Polly loved beer. She drank it on such a regular basis that it became the custom for locals to go into Cock Hotel where she lived and order a pint for themselves and a pint for Polly. When she died in 1904 she was buried in the garden of the Cock Hotel and today her gravestone can still be seen within the grounds of the hotel.

Swinton

For centuries Swinton was simply '…a small hamlet in the township of Worsley in the parish of Eccles in the hundred of Salford…' The meaning of the name dates from Viking times, 'ton' being Danish for a small farmstead and 'swine' from the Old English 'swyn'. During the 12th century much of Swinton and its neighbour, Pendlebury, were held by the Knights Hospitallers of St John of Jerusalem. The pig rearing belonged to Whalley Abbey, however, until the Dissolution of the Monasteries in 1536, after which Thurstan de Tyldesley from Wardley Hall took over. Swinton remained rural to the end of the 18th century, with agriculture and a cottage textile industry the main means of subsistence.

The township began to gain in importance during the 18th century because of coal seams and the colliery workings, which developed there as part of the Duke of Bridgewater's ambitious schemes. There were also brick fields that helped to supply the Duke of Bridgewater's demand for bricks for his canal enterprises and ventures like Brick Hall. Cotton manufacturing brought the mills to Swinton as well. The Swinton Industrial Schools opened in 1846: a collection of large brick buildings faced with stone, set in 20 acres of grounds in the angle of Chorley Road with Partington Lane. Charles Dickens visited the Schools in 1850. He was very impressed, describing them as a 'palace for pauper children...' where '...poor children were educated preparatory to apprenticeships in trade and domestic service. Girls were trained in cookery, needlework and household management; the boys learned various trades'. The Industrial Schools were considered so successful that they were deemed '...a most glorious and triumphant foreshadowing of the inestimable value of national education...' Times change though and the cotton industry declined after World War One. The Schools closed in 1925 and were demolished in 1933. Today Swinton Town Hall, built in 1938, stands on the site. The cellars remained in situ and accessible, however, and they were used as air raid shelters during World War Two.

In 1865 Swinton was separated from the parish of Eccles and came under Manchester Archdeaconry and Diocese. St Peter's Church was designed and built by Sir Gilbert Scott in 1869, on the site of an earlier church. The new church was described as being of 16th-century, Gothic-style with a tower some 112ft high, which had eight bells. The church could seat 900 people and it was a sign of Swinton's growing prosperity. St Peter's School stood close by. There was an infant's day school in Holyrood Church near Moorside, a Sunday School and Swinton Open Air School in the 1930s, which had open-sided classrooms because fresh air was considered important. The Lancashire and Yorkshire railway ran through Swinton and the company built a station there. Swinton grew rapidly. In 1851 the population was 3,132, which doubled during the next 20 years to 7,967 in 1871, and by 1901 this had nearly quadrupled to 27,005.

Swinton Local Board of Health had been established in 1867, becoming Swinton and Pendlebury Local Board of Health in 1869, although at that time Swinton was still part of Worsley township. It wasn't until 1894 that Swinton became a separate township and part of Swinton and Pendlebury Urban District. In 1907 two additional small detached parts of Worsley civil parish (which officialdom had believed to be already part of Swinton) were incorporated into Swinton civil parish within the Urban District of Swinton and Pendlebury. To this larger urban district, Clifton civil parish and a small part of Prestwich Urban District (west of the River Irwell) were added in 1933. The following year the Urban District of Swinton and Pendlebury became a municipal borough to which a small part of Worsley Urban District was added in 1995. Finally, in 1974, the Municipal Borough of Swinton and Pendlebury became part of Salford Metropolitan District.

Many of the cotton mills stood around Moorside and Moorside Park. The Dacca Twist Mill and the Simpson and Godlee Mills stood on Deans Road. Montague Burton's factory was on the East Lancashire Road. It was opened in 1938 by Lord Derby, closed in August 1973 and demolished two years later. There was also Higgins Brothers' and Jones' Foundry, near Boundary Road, and Magnesium Elektron, which produced magnesium that was much in demand during World War Two. In the 19th century mill workers would escape to Moorside Park and Victoria Park on Sundays. Swinton Wakes used to be the last week in July and the first week in August. Most families would go to Blackpool for a week's holiday, and the British Legion would arrange day trips to Southport with the additional treat of fish and chips at the Star Café.

By the early 20th century there were plenty of leisure activities in Swinton. The Lions Rugby Club stood on Partington Lane and at one time most of the rugby team were employed at Gerrard's timber merchants on Pendlebury Road. Above Gerrard's canteen there was a dance hall known as The Derby. The town had four cinemas: The Adelphi (later renamed the Essoldo) on Swinton Market Place; the Moss Empire just past Lower Sutherland Street; The Ellesmere (which had a restaurant and a dance hall as well) on the East Lancashire Road and The Plaza on Station Road. The Plaza also had a dance hall called the Swinton Palais, later the Wishing Well and then Champagne Charlie's. It subsequently became an ice skating rink.

Swinton also had quite a number of pubs in common with most industrial towns, the names bearing witness to local industries and interests, including the Farmers Arms, the Weavers Arms and the Spinners Arms, which was known locally as The Stinking Stocking because the spinners from the Acme Mill used to go for a drink in the pub and kick their clogs off to dry their damp, sweaty feet. There was The Football on Granville Street, renamed from The Dog in honour of Swinton Lions Rugby Club. A bowling green was built behind the pub in 1881. One of the oldest was the Bull's Head on Chorley Road, which dated from 1686, although the present building only dates from 1826. Here bull baiting, inquests, council meetings and club gatherings took place. These included the Watcher's Club who met in the tap room and held vigils in the graveyard to prevent body snatchers stealing recently buried corpses. Around 1928 stories of a ghost began to circulate among the regulars. It

was rumoured that '...a swirl of taffeta and a drop in temperature...' were heard and felt in the pub, but nobody had any idea of who he or she might be.

Eccles

Eccles is best known outside the north-west for its Eccles cakes. Eccles cakes are sold all over the country but some are a travesty of how a real Eccles cake should taste. Two shops in Eccles laid claim to be the original makers of Eccles cakes but their origin probably goes back to mediaeval times when they would have been made for fairs and religious festivals. In the Middle Ages sweet and savoury foods were often put into pastry cases, sometimes together (which is how Cornish pasties and mince pies originated), for ease of eating while working in the fields. One of the cake shops in Eccles belonged to William Proctor, who moved his premises in 1796; the other was Bradburn's on Church Street in Eccles, which pointedly claimed never to have moved premises. Bradburn's now no longer exist and a family named Edmonds took over the making of 'proper' Eccles cakes. They have continued the tradition that only handmade Eccles cakes can be the genuine article. Sadly for Eccles, the Edmonds moved to Ardwick, a Manchester suburb, during the 1970s, but they have set up 'the world's only purpose built Eccles cake factory' there. The cakes still have the handmade touch, although mechanisation has taken over the rolling and cutting of the puff pastry. For anyone unfortunate enough never to have tasted an Eccles cake, they are made from circular cases of puff pastry, filled with a mixture of butter, sugar, currants, mixed peel and nutmeg. The cakes are brushed with milk or water and dusted with sugar before baking to a golden brown. While this description may have dieticians recoiling in horror, a little of what you fancy does most people no harm. 'Fake' Eccles cakes are heavy on pastry, light on fruit and have a stale, stodgy, mass-produced taste. The handmade touch means that individual cakes are fresh, light and full of fruit. 'Proper' Eccles cakes are a treat to be savoured like the seven wonders of the world, and indeed someone once called Eccles cakes the eighth wonder of the world.

Not everyone is enthusiastic about Eccles cakes, however. The Puritans (early 1600s) disapproved of such goodies and denounced them as 'pagan luxuries' before trying to ban them. They didn't succeed, but, where they failed, the politically correct 21st century may succeed. In the current atmosphere of obsession with rules of conformity and desires to abolish individual and interesting foodstuffs, questions have been raised in the House of Commons as to whether Eccles cakes made with the same ingredients but not actually made in Eccles should still be called Eccles cakes and sold as such. It seems a sad thing that the Mother of

Parliaments, with so many pressing national and international matters to consider, should be so concerned with the name of a small sweet currant cake which is, after all, a part of our northern heritage.

Eccles cakes were sold at wakes and fairs throughout Lancashire and Cheshire and no wake, 'gyst-ale or guising' or fair was complete without them. Eccles Wakes were at one time quite famous. They were attended by people from neighbouring villages and hamlets and 'some dressy work-folk from Manchester'. The girls wore '...white frocks, blue stockings and clogs...' while the lads wore '...velveteen jackets and scarlet waistcoats, adorned with pearl buttons and other elegancies to match...' Horse racing and gambling were two of the main attractions, while bear baiting and cockfighting were also popular, especially after bull baiting ended in 1834. The Eccles Wakes were finally abolished in 1877, but a fair continued to be held each year.

A lady named Nelly Wood, who was born in 1792 and lived until the 1880s, recalled the Eccles Wakes during the first years of the 19th century. '...[she] *used to run in the races and won many a sixpence...there used to be...rough doings in which the women fought like good uns...bull baiting used to take place in a spot near the...Town Hall, and near the same place were stocks...men fixed in them, their faces black with passion and swearing fearfully, whilst the jeering crowd pelted them with rotten eggs, mud, and any offal on which hands could be laid. In those days...people lived on barley bread, jannocks [oat bread] and oat cakes, which accounts for the Eccles cake being considered a great luxury...'*

Another popular annual festival in Eccles was the gyst-ale (special ale brewed for guising) and guising (dressing up in costumes), which sounds not dissimilar to the Castleton Garland ceremony still practised in Derbyshire. It usually took place at the end of the marling (fertilising the soil with a mixture of carbonate of lime and clay materials) and manuring season. There is a description of guising by Frank Hird in *Lancashire Stories*, which was published in 1913:

'...*a King was chosen and, gaily dressed, and carrying garlands, the guisers set forth in a long procession. At the head a principal garland was carried, from which hung silver vessels of every variety, lent by the gentry in the neighbourhood. Each village strove to outdo its neighbour in a variety of dress and splendour of the decorated garlands, and a particularly sharp rivalry arose between Eccles and Barton...*'

Visit of King George V to Eccles in 1913. (Salford Local Studies Library)

A pamphlet published in 1778, about the rivalry between the Eccles and Barton Guisings, gives an account of the guisings of 1777. The Eccles Guising took place on 14 July when '...*a hundred men and women with pikes and swords, some dressed as Robin Hood and Little John, and others as Adam and Eve, "in a single horse-chair with an orange-tree fixed before them, and oranges growing thereon", proceeded to Barton and various parts of the village of Eccles with drums beating, trumpets sounding, music playing, and about 16 couples of morris dancers...*'

Barton held their guising on 24 September when '...*two hundred and twenty men and women, with about twenty one guns, cannon and muskets, which they began to fire as early as five o'clock in the morning, preceded by a bull with bells around his neck, marched through Eccles. This procession had a Queen, who was followed by thirty four maids of honour; there were several bands of music, twenty couples of morris dancers, banners galore, and a "grand garland drawn by good horses and proper attendance"...*'

This invasion was too much for Eccles and in October they retaliated: '...*a procession of two hundred and 16 horsemen and nearly a hundred men on foot, with a Queen who had fifty six maids of honour, "every one handsomely dressed, and with a watch by her side," could not be bettered, either in numbers or splendours by the humiliated Bartonians. The palm, therefore, lay with Eccles, and the foolish and costly rivalry ceased...*'

In the beginning there seemed to be no actual town or village of Eccles, it was the name of a parish, which included Barton upon Irwell, Clifton, Pendlebury, Pendleton and Worsley. The parish of Eccles, which also contained both Chat Moss and Trafford Moss in the Middle Ages,

Monks Hall, Eccles, in 1931. (Manchester Archives and Local Studies Library, Central Library)

belonged to Whalley Abbey from the mediaeval period until the Dissolution of the Monasteries in 1536. What became the village and then the town of Eccles was originally part of Barton upon Irwell. However, a church in Eccles is said to have existed in AD 1111 so it maybe that the actual place of Eccles has existed for the best part of 1,000 years, at least; certainly Eccles village is mentioned in 13th-century charters. There are also the remains of an old Saxon cross (found near the church during the building of the ship canal in the 1890s), which may have originally stood in the centre of the village or marked the village boundaries.

From 1192 there is a deed showing that Lady Edith de Barton and Robert de Gresley gave a moiety (portion; usually half) of the church with land and two pastures to Geoffrey de Byron, who was the parson at that time. Her grandson sold the advowson (right to choose the parson or vicar) of Eccles to John de Lacy, Constable of Chester. De Lacy was killed fighting alongside Richard Coeur de Lion during the Crusade against Tyre in Syria, but he gave Eccles to the monastery of Stanlaw on the Mersey, which later moved to the Whalley. Granges and tithe barns were built during the monastic period of Eccles, one of which almost certainly stood on the site of Monks Hall near to St Mary's Church.

The present St Mary's Church appears to have been founded in 1368, though the earliest surviving part is St Katharine's Chapel, built around 1450 but rebuilt in 1862–3. The present church is 16th-century with

St Mary's Church, Eccles, in 1950. (Manchester Archives and Local Studies Library, Central Library)

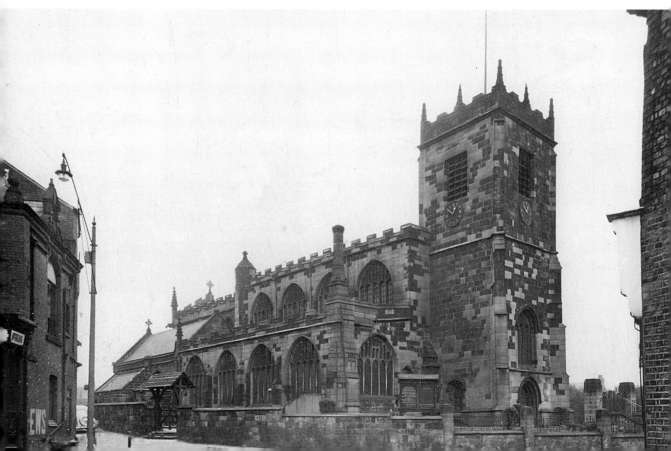

The tomb of Richard and Dorothy Brereton, 1952. (Manchester Archives and Local Studies Library, Central Library)

traces of a 14th-century building, and the tower is 15th-century. Repairs were effected in the 18th and 19th centuries, and in 1907 the badly decayed sandstone fabric was faced. Inside the church there is a Dauntesey family brass on the south side of the chancel arch and there is the Brereton family tomb. The tomb is an 'altar tomb' on which lies the effigy of a knight in full armour and beside him lies his wife in Elizabethan dress. The tragic inscription, which is in Latin, and runs around the edge of the tomb and reads:

'Here lie the bodies of Richard Brereton de Tatton and Worsley Esqre, and of Dorothy, his wife, daughter of Richard Egerton de Ridley, knight: and Richard, their son; which Richard died 17 December 1598, and the said Dorothy died 4 April 1639. And the said Richard, their son, who was an infant, died in 1575. And the said Dorothy caused this monument to be made in 1600.'

Richard, their son, was an only child and with him died the family line. When Richard Senior died he left Worsley Old Hall to Thomas Egerton, Dorothy's half brother, from whom the Dukes of Bridgewater were directly descended. A 19th-century writer summed up the pathos '...the passing of that little life set gigantic forces in motion two hundred years later...'

By the end of the 18th century '...*the agriculture of the parish is chiefly confined to grazing, and would be ...benefitted by draining...but the tax upon brick, a most essential article in this process, has been a very great hindrance....the use of lime (imported from Wales, and brought by inland navigations to the neighbourhood of our collieries) has become very general in the improvement of the meadow and pasture lands...and on all lands properly drained, it has nearly superceded the use of marl...'*

During the 1760s the Duke of Bridgewater had built-up the brick-making industry and established brick kilns in the neighbouring Worsley locality for his canal enterprises and the construction of Brick Hall. Did he perhaps try to help by offering brick for drainage or did he simply consider that Eccles was not his problem?

A writer of 1795 justified the canals by his description of the roads before they had to seriously compete with the railways and waterways: *'...the roads...are becoming an object of very general and serious concern. To make and preserve these...is indispensable for the interests of agriculture and commerce. Much labour, and a very great expense of money, have been expended on the roads...but they still remain in a very indifferent state, and from one plain and obvious cause, the immoderate weights drawn in wagons and carts. To prevent this, vain and useless are all the regulations of weighing machines: and the encouragement of broad and rolling wheels still increases the evil, which must soon destroy all the best roads of Great Britain, and by their irresistible crush exhaust all the ballast or gravel... required to repair the mischief they occasion...'*

Since little seems to have changed, these sentiments are no doubt shared by those responsible for maintaining the modern roads.

The growth of the cotton mills and the textile industry in the late 18th and the 19th centuries meant plenty of new jobs for the people of Eccles but 'it is...the...plan of providence that there shall be no good without its attendant inconvenience...' The attendant inconvenience in this case was the girls and women who went out to work; a subject on which the jury is still out in the 21st century. It meant that *'...females are wholly uninstructed in sewing, knitting, and other domestic affairs, requisite to make them notable and frugal wives and mothers...this a very great misfortune...as is sadly proved by a comparison of the families of labourers in husbandry [farming], and those of manufacturers in general. In the former we meet with neatness, cleanliness and comfort; in the latter with filth, rags and poverty; although their wages may be nearly double to those of the husbandman...'*

Jonathan Aiken wrote, in 1795, that in Eccles parish there was also considerable unease about children working in the mills and the conditions that they endured.

'...children of very tender age are employed; many of them collected from workhouses in London and Westminster, and transported in crowds, as apprentices to masters resident many hundred miles distant, where they serve unknown, unprotected, and forgotten by those to whose

Bridgewater Canal, Monton, Eccles, in 1900. (Manchester Archives and Local Studies Library, Central Library)

care nature or the laws had consigned them. These children are usually too long confined to work in close rooms, often during the whole night; the air they breathe from the oil etc employed in the machinery, and other circumstances, is injurious; little regards is paid to their cleanliness and frequent change from warm and dense to a cold and thin atmosphere, are predisposing causes to sickness and disability, and particularly to the epidemic fever which is so generally to be met with in these factories. It is also much to be questioned, if society does not receive detriment from the manner in which children are thus employed during their years...'

The population of Eccles parish almost doubled between 1830, when it was 23,331, and 1851, by which time it had risen to 40,493. About a tenth of these lived in the village of Eccles. Industries included silk weaving; cotton spinning and weaving; calico printing; bleaching; coal mining and a factory that manufactured steam locomotives. The Manchester–Liverpool railway and the Manchester–Bolton railway both passed through. At the opening of the Manchester–Liverpool railway there was a tragic accident and Mr William Huskisson MP and President of the Board of Trade was run over by a train. He had stumbled from a carriage on an embankment, where there was only room to stand between the two sets of railway lines, panicked, and fell in front of an oncoming train. He suffered severe leg injuries and was carried to the vicarage in

Botanic Beer and Porter Stores, c.1894. (Manchester Archives and Local Studies Library, Central Library)

Eccles where, despite devoted nursing by the vicar's wife, he died five days later.

In 1853 Eccles was described as a 'pleasant village'. Eccles Cross (the centre of the village) was surrounded by houses and small shops, including the Old Thatch (rumoured to have been built in 1094), which sold herb beer and Eccles cakes. It was demolished in the early years of the 20th century, however, and Williams and Deacons Bank was built on the site in 1915. Near to the church there was a Grammar School. There was also an infant school, about half a dozen day schools attached to various chapels, and a Sunday School. Eccles Town Hall was built in 1881 on the site of a former cock pit. There was a company of volunteers (militia) that had been raised at Eccles in 1797. The Barton, Eccles, Winton and Monton Local Board of Health '… was established in 1854 for the northern part of Barton upon Irwell township…in 1892, together with a small part of Worsley township, the Board became largely…the same as that of the Borough of Eccles… [which] was in Barton upon Irwell Poor Law Union…' (GMCRO).

By the end of the 19th century, Eccles had public baths, a library, parks, sewage works, a cemetery, electricity, a railway station, a fire station and tramways. The Town Hall was built in 1881 on the site of the old cock pit. A Charter of Incorporation was granted in 1892 and the Council

The Chains in Eccles Old Road in Eccles, c.1896.

Methodist Chapel, Eccles New Road, in 1930. (Manchester Archives and Local Studies Library, Central Library)

Congregational
Church, Eccles,
in 1973.
(Manchester
Archives and
Local Studies
Library, Central
Library)

Clifton Hall in
Eccles,
demolished in
1936, from an
illustration in
1860.
(Manchester
Archives and
Local Studies
Library, Central
Library)

Clifton Hall in 1908. (Manchester Archives and Local Studies Library, Central Library)

Chamber and Police Courts were built in 1899. Eccles Picture Palace opened in 1912 and later became the Empire Picture Palace. It did not survive the onset of the television age and by 1991 had become a carpet showroom. Barton Moss civil parish and part of Worsley Urban District were added to Eccles in 1933, and in 1961 a fraction of Eccles Borough was added to Salford Borough; then finally, in 1974, Eccles Borough became part of Salford Metropolitan District.

Clifton

This parish is one of the smaller parishes in the north-east of what is now the City of Salford, another settlement that originated in Viking times and

St Anne's Church, Clifton, in 1935. (Manchester Archives and Local Studies Library, Central Library)

probably took its name from being the farmstead on a steep hill. It lay in a good coal mining area on the old Manchester to Bolton Road. Clifton was the 'third part' of the Borough of Swinton and Pendlebury and was mentioned in a Pipe Roll of 1151. It was held by several families in turn, including the de Traffords and the de Hollands. Ancient Clifton Hall was home to the de Hollands.

Robert Ainsworth, a scholar who compiled a well-known Latin dictionary, was born in Clifton village in 1660. Another well-known family of Clifton were the Pilkingtons. They had large coal mining interests in the area and were renowned for their tile-producing factory, as well as playing an important part in establishing the Royal Lancastrian pottery. Lawrence Pilkington wrote prose and poetry including two novels based on Clifton village. In the mid-18th century James Brindley, the engineer who built the underground canal system at Worsley, was called in to solve a flooding problem in one of the local mines, which he did by diverting water through a tunnel to the waterwheel at Wet Earth Colliery.

In 1830 the population was 1,168 and had risen slightly by 1853 to 1,647. Clifton was linked to the railways by this time, with the East Lancashire railway to Bury meeting the Lancashire and Yorkshire line to Bolton in the town. The railway station, however, was on the Lancashire

and Yorkshire railway. In 1873 the land was still largely pasture, St Anne's Church was still not built and services were being conducted in a former school. There was also a National School and an Infant's School. Most of Clifton was added to Swinton Urban District Council in 1933, and in 1934 Swinton and Pendlebury became a municipal borough.

Pendlebury

Pendlebury, in the ecclesiastical parish of Eccles, was the 'second part' of the Borough of Swinton and Pendlebury. The name means that is was originally a fortified place (or manor) on a hill or the edge of a hill, and the earliest records of the place go back 1201 when it was linked with the manor of nearby Shoresworth. Early historians were at pains to point out that it should not be confused with Pendlebury near Clitheroe, a little further to the north. Agecroft Hall, originally built about 1390 and rebuilt during the early 16th century, lay in Pendlebury. The area of Pendlebury known as Shoresworth became part of Salford Borough in 1853 and was added to Pendleton in 1883. The remainder of Pendlebury was included with the Swinton Local Board of Health area from 1867, and in 1869 this became the Swinton and Pendlebury Local Board of Health. Swinton and Pendlebury Urban District came into being in 1894, and in 1934 the Urban District of Swinton and Pendlebury became a municipal borough. Finally, in 1974, the Municipal Borough of Swinton and Pendlebury became part of Salford Metropolitan District.

The township was smaller, more rural and had a higher location than Swinton. In 1830 Pendlebury had a population of 1,047, which had increased a little by 1853. At this time most of the population worked in the local collieries. The River Irwell and Manchester, Bury and Bolton Canal ran past the eastern side of the town. Pendlebury lay just on the

other side of the railway to Swinton, but the nearest railway station was at Clifton Junction. By 1873 cotton manufacture and coal mining were the main industries, and the population had grown to 5,163. The main landowners were now Edward Heywood and Andrew Knowles. Spring Field, one of the more eminent houses, was the family home of Thomas Entwistle.

St John's Church, was built of plain stone in 1842, followed by Christ Church, built, in 1859, of stone in the early-English style. Each church had a tower with a single bell. Christ Church had its own school and there were National Schools for boys, girls and infants connected with St John's. Pendlebury was close enough to Swinton to share in its dance halls and cinemas, though Pendlebury could boast one cinema of its own called The Palace, which lay on Bolton Road and was known locally as The Bug. There was a tripe factory in Pendlebury. Tripe is the lining of a sheep's stomach and the eyes of non-northern folk have been known to glaze in horror at the thought, but tripe (raw or cooked) and onions have long been considered a cheap and nourishing delicacy in Lancashire. However, perhaps Pendlebury's main claim to fame is that it was the home of L.S. Lowry for 40 years.

Lawrence Stephen Lowry was the only child of Irish parents and was born in Rusholme. He was educated at a school in Victoria Park and then attended Manchester College of Art and Salford School of Art. Afterwards Lowry lived in Pendlebury, becoming renowned for his paintings of the Salford and Manchester millscapes peopled by small stick-like figures, who were immortalized in the popular song '*Matchstick Men...and matchstick cats and dogs..*' but it was the scenes painted on and around Bolton Road that made him famous.

Pendleton

Pendleton was a larger township and closer to Manchester than Pendlebury, though it shares a similar name, meaning the farmstead on the hill. To the north lay Hyle Wood. In the wood there was '...an oblong hillock of sand...', which legend says was a Viking burial tumulus. Prior to 1830 this tumulus had been tree-covered. It is more likely to have been of Saxon origin, but they were the people defeated by the Vikings in the ninth century. Pendleton lay within Eccles ecclesiastical parish and the area covered by Salford Poor Law Union. In 1853 Pendleton became a part of Salford Borough, and in 1883 Shoresworth, a small detached part of Pendlebury township, became part of Pendleton township. There was an exchange of lands in the Davyhulme area with Barton upon Irwell in 1892 and later, in 1961, a small part of Eccles Borough was added to Pendleton (GMCRO).

Opposite: *St Thomas's Church, Pendleton in 1910. (Manchester Archives and Local Studies Library, Central Library)*

The town stood in an elevated position with good views and was a popular location with mill owners, manufacturers and merchants, who did not wish to live in the dire industrial conditions that they had created in Manchester. These included James Touchet, the local squire, of Broom House, B.A. Heywood, who lived at Clermont; Highfield Hall, the seat of Mrs Withington, and Hope House, the home of Edward Hobson. There were '... four superior private and boarding schools...' (attesting to a wealthy element among the population), and there was also a literary society. Pendleton Old Hall had improved land, which was important for

A Clog maker in Pendleton in 1956. (Manchester Archives and Local Studies Library, Central Library)

Pendleton station and canal in 1966. (Manchester Archives and Local Studies Library, Central Library)

water and mineral rights. New Hall farm and dairy were demolished in
1926 and the Irwell Valley School now stands on the site.

Pendleton had a Turnpike Trust, which had toll bars on Eccles Old
Road and Bolton Road until 1870. The Woolpack Inn stood at the
junction of these two roads. It had two drinking troughs for horses and a
drinking fountain with chained metal cups for travellers. In the Pendleton
area there were extensive coal seams and, by 1841, there were two cotton
mills in the town. While in 1780 Pendleton was described as a 'small rural

West Calvinist Chapel, Pendleton, in 1878. (Manchester Archives and Local Studies Library, Central Library)

village', the population in 1801 was 3,611, which rose steadily to 4,805 in 1811, 5,948 in 1821 and up to 8,435 by 1831, an increase of nearly two and half times within 30 years. St Thomas's Church was built in 1776, '...a neat brick building with a turret and a bell...' and there were chapels for Wesleyans, Methodists and Independents. The schools seemed numerous and included '...six Dame schools, eight common schools and

'Morning Star', Pendleton, in 1967. (Manchester Archives and Local Studies Library, Central Library)

An aerial view of Hope Hospital, 1925. (Manchester Archives and Local Studies Library, Central Library)

an infants school...' Dame schools were so called because they were usually run by one woman using her home as a school. Some were excellent, others questionable, but for 18th and early 19th-century working class children any education was better than none.

Hope Hospital in Pendleton, near Eccles New Road, opened in 1882 as Salford Union Infirmary or Workhouse. The hospital has gradually expanded over the years and has become well-known for the treatment of skin and stomach problems.

Pendleton also has one or two more gruesome aspects to its history. On 8 September 1817 a whole family were executed at Lancaster Castle for robbery and a 'memorable murder' at a house, which stood close to the delightfully named Three-Nooked Field near the Maypole Inn on Whit Lane and the Colliery. Coincidentally, Lancaster Prison had a record number of executions that took place there in 1817, but even in those times the execution of a family was unprecedented. There was much excitement and unrest because many people believed that the four: James Ashcroft, his son James, his brother David, and his brother-in-law Thomas Holden, were innocent despite their conviction for robbery with violence and murder. There was, however, no reprieve forthcoming and all four paid the supreme penalty.

Almost 60 years before another Pendleton murderer, John Grindred, had paid the supreme penalty when he was gibbeted on Pendleton Moor for poisoning his wife and two children in 1759. The site was known as Cross Lane by the late 19th century and also stood close to Three-Nooked Field. William Harrison Ainsworth, the celebrated Salford novelist, wrote a short epic poem in 17 stanzas called *Old Grindred's Ghost*, which described how Grindred's skeleton would take midnight walks to '...dispel wetness and weariness occasioned by long suspension...' One dark wet night this story was told to a traveller who had stopped at a nearby inn (probably The Maypole) soon after the execution. The traveller just laughed in disbelief and struck a wager for '...a rump and a dozen...' that he would walk alone to the gibbet after midnight and talk to the skeleton, and if it replied he would lose his bet. The outcome is best related through a few selected stanzas from the poem:

'...*though dark as could be yet he thought he could see*
the skeleton hanging on high
the gibbet it creaked, and the rusty chains squeaked
and a screech-owl flew solemnly by

the heavy rain pattered, the hollow bones clattered, the traveller's
teeth chattered - with cold - not with fright
the wind it blew lustily, piercingly, gustily
certainly not an agreeable night!

Ho! Grindred, old fellow! thus loudly did bellow
the traveller mellow, "how are ye, my blade?"
"I'm cold and I'm dreary; I'm wet and I'm weary
but soon I'll be near ye" the skeleton said

the grisly bones rattled, and with the chains battled,
the gibbet appallingly shook;
on the ground something stirred, but no more the man heard
to his heels on the instant he took

over moorland he dashed, and through quagmire he splashed
his pace never daring to slack
till the hostel he neared, for greatly he feared
Old Grindred would leap on his back

his wager he lost, and a trifle it cost,
but that which annoyed him the most,
was to find out too late, that certain as fate,
the landlord had acted the ghost,'

(Ainsworth, William Harrison. *Old Grindred's Ghost*. c.1830s.)

Chat Moss

The story of Chat Moss is curious and almost eerie. Mosses (a prettier name than peat bogs) are common in north-west England, a combination of underground springs, poor drainage and the sphagnum moss, which was laid down as a result of climate change about 5,000 years ago. The best known moss is Lindow Moss in neighbouring Cheshire in which 'Lindow Man' was found. Pete Moss, as he was nicknamed by pathologists who examined his body, had been strangled, stabbed and drowned (according to the Celtic triple murder ritual for sacrificial victims) before his body was cast into the moss 2,500 years ago as an offering to the Gods. The treacherous inhospitable nature of English mosses and legends of the unearthly spirits that were supposed to inhabit them led to their avoidance by those living in the locality. Such areas remained shunned waste ground for centuries.

Chat Moss was no exception until it quite literally erupted into the public consciousness. John Leland, the Tudor historiographer of Henry VIII, describes how, in 1526 '...*a great eruption [of Chat Moss]...choked the Glazebrook, covered sixty acres of arable land each side...overflowed the dam of Culcheth [Corn] Mill and prevented passage of the ferry at Hollinfare for some days...*' Contemporary 16th-century accounts tell of the force of the eruption. '...[Chat Moss]... *is a ii or iii mile in bredthe...Gleasebroke river cummith with in lesse than a mile of Morley Hawle...flete and a notter broke...cummith in to Gleasebrook and Glasebrook goith in to Mers [ey]...Chateley More [Chat Moss] a v mile yn length sum brast up with in a mile of Morley Haul, and [de]stroied much grounde with mosse thereabou[t], and destroyed much fresch water fische th[ere]about, first corrupting with stin[k]ing water Glasebrook, and so Glasebrook car[ried] stinking water and mosse in to Mersey water and Mersey corrupted carri the roulling mosse part to the shores of Wa[les], part to the Ile of Man, and sum in Ireland. In the very top of Chatemore [Chat Moss] where the mosse was hyest and broke is no[w] a fair plain valley as was in tymes past an a rille runnill in hit and peaces of smaul trees be found in the botom...*' Sixteenth-century spelling and grammar were not standardized, but the sense of the scale of destruction is apparent and it is interesting that the writer describes a valley as there may have been in 'tymes past', a past nearly 5,000 years before.

There were several accounts of the damage caused:
'...*with breking up of abundance of waters yn hit did much hurte to landis thereabout and rivers with wandering mosse and corrupt water...*'
'...*thanket be to God that no crystyn body was pisshed [perished], but they lost ther godes in ther howss, with ther corne and hey in ther bernes, some swyne and dogs drow[n]yd...*'

'...in thys mosse and water brake owtt...in ye morning, abowt vii of ye clock...and some howss stood in water to ye eysing [eaves]...'

Daniel Defoe was less than complimentary about Chat Moss when he visited the area in the early years of the 19th century. He wrote:

'...it stretched...for five or six miles, the surface looked black and dirty...and it was...indeed frightful to think of, for it would bear neither horse nor man, unless in an exceedingly dry season, and then so as not be travelled over with safety...'

In 1805 William Roscoe leased Chat Moss for a period of 92 years and started reclamation work. He began marling using a portable railway with the 'weight spread over a large surface area' to carry the truck loads of marl. Robert Stannard introduced an improved portable railway system in 1816, which worked well, but in 1821 Roscoe went bankrupt and Stannard ceased his involvement. Roscoe's leasehold was sold and in 1823 the construction of the Liverpool and Manchester railway across the Moss was begun by '...floating of the railway on a brushwood base, laid herringbone fashion... the warp and weft of the trees of Botany Bay wood used...'

The engineers, who finally managed to successfully build nearly five miles of the Liverpool and Manchester railway over '...this black and spongy tract...' in 1830, echoed Defoe's thoughts. Chat Moss '...had quick and faithless depths...' and it was '...doubted whether a road was practicable over this soft and watery expanse upon many parts of which it was unsafe to tread...' The railway itself was considered '...a great triumph of engineering...'

Chat Moss, which lies not far from Irlam and Cadishead, was eventually fully reclaimed in the 20th century. The Moss's '...quick and faithless depths...', in fact, varied between 24 and 30ft deep and reclamation was no easy task. However, whatever secrets Chat Moss held in its depths were not relinquished and no one will ever know what lay beneath or what became of its unearthly inhabitants.

Cadishead

Irlam and Cadishead are usually bracketed together but they are in fact quite separate places, in the most westerly part of the 'new' Salford. Until the 19th century both were mainly remote areas of Chat Moss before it was drained and reclaimed. There seems to be no trace for the name Cadishead but there is a small nocturnal insect, which lives near water, called a caddis-fly, the larvae of which is simply known as a caddis. Head can simply mean a small promontory. Other historical sources, however, suggest that the meaning is that of a '...dwelling or a fold by the stream of a man called Cada...'

Liverpool Road, from a postcard of Cadishead, c.1907.

The first mention of Cadishead comes in AD 1212, when Gilbert Notton rented (held in theynage) 'Cadwalensate' or 'Cadewalsate' from King John. Spellings could be very individual in the 13th century. Before that, Cadishead had been '...held by serjeanty of carpentry with Edwin as tenant...' Soon after 1212, Cadishead was grated to the monks of Whalley Abbey by William and Agnes de Ferrers. In 1348, however, the theynage rent was still being charged to the Abbot of Whalley and was only waived when he proved that he held the alms through his charter agreement with de Ferrers. By 1666 hearth tax returns show that Cadishead had 28 hearths, of which 11 (nearly half) belonged to Thomas Holcroft.

Work on reclaiming Chat Moss did not begin until 1805 and it was this reclamation that first enabled Cadishead to grow. Even so, progress was initially slow, and as late as 1853 Cadishead was still a '...small hamlet whose population is principally engaged in manufactures...'

Cadishead fought a brief 'civil war' with Irlam in 1817, which lasted four weeks and left 98 people dead and 124 injured (see Irlam). Cadishead was smaller and poorer than Irlam, but the Mayor of Irlam, James Herbert, had decided that a subsection of Salford Borough law had been broken and consequently declared war on Cadishead.

St Mary's Church was not built until 1929 and prior to that the local congregation worshipped in a temporary building known as the 'tin church' due to the amount of corrugated iron used in its construction. The new church was built by Brew Brothers of Moss Lane, Cadishead, and consecrated on 2 February 1929, the day of the Festival of the Lambs in the old agricultural calendar. The tower was not built due to a design amendment and the East Wall was not fully completed until 1968. The East Window, which symbolises the Epiphany, is dedicated as a war memorial to both World Wars, and the Garden of Remembrance was consecrated in 1980.

The chief source of employment in Cadishead was the Co-operative Soap Works, with many also working at the neighbouring Irlam Steel Works until they closed down in 1979. Today part of the Irlam Industrial Estate is in Cadishead. The current population of the town is about 10,000. Cadishead is said to have some affordable house prices and a number of small housing estates have been built in recent years. Cadishead's emblem is a blue rose on a yellow background and the local rugby team are called the Cadishead Rhinos.

Irlam

The town was known as a village in 1190, which went by the name of Urwelham from 'urre', an enclosure, and 'wella', a winding stream. Ham is from the Danish word for a small village. By around 1212 the name had mutated to Irrewilham and it was held by the de Irlam family, whose seat was the ancient Irlam Hall. However, by 1688 Irlam Hall was the home of Thomas Lathom, who was instrumental in bringing William of Orange to be King of England and to reign jointly with Queen Mary after the 'Bloodless Revolution', which had forced the Catholic James II to flee England for the Continent.

In 1666 hearth tax returns show that there were 37 hearths in Irlam, of which Mr Lathom owned six. There were some curious field names including Eaves, Bosses, Poos, Sparth and Morley Croft. The latter may have been a reference to a bleaching croft. Irlam was divided among several tenants, and there was an Irlam surname in the district down to the 18th century. By this time the Lathoms of Irlam also had an estate at Hawthorn near Wilmslow, and Irlam Hall was owned by John Greaves, a wealthy merchant and a partner, as a banker, of Sir Robert Peel.

In 1817 Irlam declared war on its neighbour, Cadishead, over broken local government regulations. This petty squabble, which caused a small scale 'civil war', would have been amusing had it not been for the deadly seriousness with which both sides fought, quite literally. The 'war' raged for 29 days, from 31 August to 28 September 1817, before it was agreed that Mayor James Herbert of Irlam and Mayor Mr Cavanner of Cadishead should develop new regulations that were a workable compromise.

Much of Irlam belonged to Lancashire until 1974. The area was mostly swampy moss until the draining and reclamation of Chat Moss during the early years of the 19th century. Some areas remain remote today, especially that around Woolden Hall. In 1894 Irlam Urban District was formed from the area of Barton upon Irwell, and the Manchester Ship Canal, which had such an effect on the area, opened. In addition, a diversion of the Liverpool–Manchester railway was necessitated by the construction of the ship canal and a new station had to be built at Irlam. Two years later, in 1896, a part of Irlam township was added to Barton Moss and there were land exchanges between Irlam Urban District and Flixton, followed, in 1920, by similar exchanges with Carrington and Partington. In 1933 there were more land exchanges, this time with Worsley, and in 1969 with Golborne Urban District and Rixton with Glazebrook, before becoming part of Salford Metropolitan District in 1974.

A good deal of industrial development took place along the banks of the ship canal and this included the Irlam Steelworks, which opened in 1910 and were a major employer in the area until their closure in 1979. An industrial estate now stands on the former site of the steelworks. Irlam did not experience the dramatic population rise of many places. In 1853 it was dismissed as just a hamlet, and by 1901 the population was still only 4,000, athough by the outbreak of World War Two it had reached 14,600. In 1974, when Irlam became part of Salford, the population was only just over 20,500. Irlam has one large school providing secondary education, which is named Irlam and Cadishead Community High School (formerly Irlam High School). There are swimming baths and sports teams include Irlam Town Football Club and Irlam Indians Roller Hockey Club. The symbol of Irlam is still the Red Rose.

Irlam o' th' Heights
Although the place name is similar to Irlam, the township is, as the name suggests, at a higher altitude. However, it is not connected with Irlam but is situated within the Pendlebury and Pendleton townships.

Barton upon Irwell
The name suggests that Barton, usually called Barton upon Irwell to distinguish it from other places of the same name, began life as a fenced farmstead beside the River Irwell. Most of Barton lies on the north side of the Irwell; the area on the southern side forms Davyhulme, which is part of Flixton. In 1894 the Manchester Ship Canal replaced the Irwell as the boundary of Barton. To the south-west of the original Barton village lay Chat Moss, hence the township name of Barton Moss, which included Eccles, Irlam and Davyhulme. The actual village of Barton Moss was very small, no more than a hamlet, whose population in 1901 was just 234 people. In 1666 hearth tax returns show that Barton had 101 taxable hearths, which included those of George Legh (14), Thomas Sorocold (13) and John Barlow (6). There were also some quaint field names such as Neckars, Scythy Field, Hoasefield and Shoe Broad. Barton Old Hall was a black and white timbered building of the Tudor period, which passed to Edmund Trafford through his marriage to Anne Booth.

Barton upon Irwell's proximity to the Manchester and Liverpool railway and the Bridgewater Canal contributed significantly to the town becoming a cotton manufacturing area. As one 19th century writer put it: '...the facilities of passenger traffic offered...have induced several of the opulent classes of Manchester to reside here, and this has tended to materially improve the township...' St Catherine's Church was built shortly before 1853 and there were several chapels of various denominations including Barton Wesleyan Chapel, which was built with its own schoolroom in 1796. Between 1865–68 All Saints' Church on Barton Road was designed and built in Victorian high-Gothic style by the distinguished architect Edward Pugin.

The village of Patricroft immediately adjoined Barton and it was in

Patricroft that the extensive iron foundry of Nasmyth, Gaskell and Co were situated. James Nasmyth invented the industrial steam hammer, which could forge large pieces of machinery. Queen Victoria visited the Foundry in 1853. By the end of the 19th century there were six iron foundries in Patricroft, including the Vulcan Works, and several cotton mills such as the Bridgewater Mill. The population of Patricroft and Barton in 1851 was 7,936 of which 3,193 lived in Barton. Sometime before 1849 a workhouse had been built on Green Lane in Patricroft to accommodate 100 inmates, but this was extended in 1853 to house 230 people and an infirmary was added in 1879–80.

Barton, of course, was most noted for the Barton Aqueduct, where 'ships sailed over ships', built in 1765 by James Brindley, who disliked lock systems, to carry the Duke of Bridgewater's canal over the River Irwell. It was a unique feat of engineering skill, which many had believed could not be done. The aqueduct was moved by Eccles Town Council during the building of the Manchester Ship Canal, or the Big Ditch as it was known locally, and in 1896 it was placed where it still stands today; but, although it has been preserved, it is out of its true context. The aqueduct was replaced by Barton Swing Aqueduct, designed and built by Edward Leader-Williams, which was operated by hydraulics from the canal tower. The 234ft long trough of the aqueduct held 800 tons of water held in by gates at each end. One strangely surreal aspect of the ship canal was that, because of its nature, huge ships would appear to be gliding across the fields.

A millscape at Irlam.
(Lancashire Steel
Company), 1921.

Salford Folk

Salford has a number of well-known personalities associated with the city and its townships; some past, some present, some born and bred in Salford, others passing through. This section gives details of Salford folk, some well-known, some not so well-known, to people a landscape of facts and figures and historical descriptions, and to give a personal touch, a glimpse behind the anonymous façades of the houses. There is a larger section on the astronomer William Crabtree and the Revd Cowherd and Joseph Brotherton and also a selection of others who, in their own way, have made their mark, both locally and nationally, on the pages of history.

William Crabtree and the Transit of Venus
William Crabtree was born in Salford in 1610, the son of John Crabtree and Isabel Pendleton. He was educated at Manchester Grammar School before becoming a cloth merchant, or chapman, who travelled around delivering yarn and buying woven cloth from farms and cottages, where yarn was spun on a spinning wheel and cloth was woven on a handloom. Crabtree prospered as a draper and lived at the family home in Broughton until his marriage. He married Elizabeth Pendleton (1612–1644) and he built his own house, which he named Broughton Spout, in the Lower Broughton area. He and Elizabeth had four children: three daughters and a son named William, who was born on 25 January 1640.

William Crabtree was comfortable financially and this meant that he could indulge his passion for astronomy. He had a telescope and astronomer's cross staff, and he spent a great deal of time observing the stars and the planets and calculating his observations, some of which disproved popular astronomical theories of the time. His reference books included those by Johannes Keppler on planetary motions and Galileo on the science of astronomy.

In 1636 Crabtree met Jeremiah Horrocks, a young teacher and astronomer living and working at Much Hoole near Chorley. Not many of Crabtree's manuscripts have survived but there is a small collection in the Royal Greenwich Observatory archives, held by Cambridge University Library, which includes observations of a lunar eclipse that occurred on 10 December 1638. Crabtree's planetary observations from August 1636–September 1638 were printed in John Wallace's edition of *Jeremiae Horrocci,* published in 1673. Comparing notes with Crabtree enabled Horrocks to work out the actual course between Venus, the

Earth and the Sun. He was then able to calculate the transit of Venus, when the planet passes directly between the Earth and the Sun, and on 26 October 1639 realised that the next one was due to take place on 24 November that year. Johannes Keppler, a contemporary astronomer, had already spotted a transit in 1631 but had not realised that the transits came in pairs eight years apart. Horrocks then worked out future transits, including the most recent one that took place on 8 June 2004.

Horrocks wrote excitedly to Crabtree shortly before the 1639 transit: '…I beseech you, therefore, with all thy strength to attend diligently with a telescope'. The 24 November was a Sunday and fortunately a sunny day. Instead of observing religious practices, as was usual, both men sat in their respective homes and, at around 3.15pm, observed Venus passing in front of the sun; a tiny black dot, barely visible. By comparing their records of the moment when Venus began its transit, the two men were able to calculate distances between other astronomical bodies and discovered vital information about the courses of other planets as they orbited the sun. Their work laid the foundations for the study of the planetary motions.

In 1640 Crabtree visited William Gascoigne, who also lived and worked in the vicinity, and reported back to Horrocks on Gascoigne's invention of a micrometer, which gave effective telescopic sights. Horrocks died suddenly and unexpectedly in 1641. This was a great loss to Crabtree who described Horrocks as 'my friend and second self'. The two men had worked together well and agreed on many matters including Keppler's theories of planetary motion. In 1642, on 21 June, Crabtree wrote to William Gascoigne and described Horrocks's lunar theory, not knowing at the time that his letter would become a major historical record.

By this time Crabtree himself was 'sick in body' and he died towards the end of July in 1644. He was buried in Manchester and his will was proved the following year. In June 2004 a commemorative plaque to William Crabtree was unveiled at the site believed to have been where his house stood at the junction of Lower Broughton Road and Priory Grove.

Revd William Cowherd and the establishment of Vegetarianism
In 1809 the aptly named Revd Cowherd founded the Bible Christian Church in Salford, a break-away church from the Swedenborgian New Church in King Street, and insisted that his congregation take a vow that they would not eat meat. Similar vegetarian chapels were established in Ancoats and Hulme. Vegetarianism, advocated by the Greek mathematician Pythagoras 2,500 years ago, is based on the principle that

'...there is a kinship of all nature...' The main reason, initially, for Mancunians and Salfordians being receptive to the idea was probably due more to economics than high principles. Many could not afford meat anyway and it was an ideal way of saving face to say that they did not eat meat because of their religious beliefs. However, the movement grew in popularity and this was almost certainly the period when that standard of Lancashire cookery, potato pie, became a staple part of the diet. Potato pie suppers are still held, often at charity fundraising events.

The Sedenborgian Church, in 1860, where Revd Cowherd's break away church was formed from. (Manchester Archives and Local Studies Library, Central Library)

William Cowherd died in 1816 and was buried in the King Street churchyard. Today the church has gone but the burials in the graveyard were not moved. A car park currently lies over the graves and a few of the headstones are just visible through the asphalt. The car park fronts Greengate and Irwell factory. Cowherd's work was carried on by his successor, Pastor Joseph Brotherton, who became Salford's first MP in 1832, after the Reform Act was passed. In 1847 he founded the Vegetarian Society, which elected James Simpson, of Cowherd's Bible Christian Church, as its first president. His father-in-law's sister, Martha Harvey, was married to Joseph Brotherton and she wrote the first vegetarian cookery book. One of the society's slogans was 'live and let live'. The first AGM took place at Manchester's Hayward's Hotel and 232 people attended the vegetarian dinner given afterwards. During the 1850s Salford Council became the first council in the world to hold a vegetarian banquet.

After Joseph Brotherton died in 1857, the Revd James Clark, who was pastor at the Bible Christian Church for nearly half a century, became secretary of the Vegetarian Society and also founded the International Vegetarian Union, which had strong links with the American Vegetarian

Society founded in 1861 by the Revd William Metcalfe, a member of the Bible Christian Church who had emigrated in 1817. However, the 20th century brought a change in fortunes. The Bible Christian Church moved to Cross Lane but by 1930, unable to attract sufficient numbers of vegetarians, it merged with Pendleton Unitarian Church.

(For further information see: Antrobus, Derek. *A Guiltless Feast*. Salford City Council, *c*.2000.)

Greenwood, Walter (1903–1974)

This very northern writer was born in Ellor Street, Salford, the area that he called Hanky Park, and educated at Langworthy Road Council School, which he left at the age of 13. Most of his reading and studying was done in Salford Library and his letters and manuscripts are deposited with Salford University. He tried a number of jobs, earning a pittance, and then, to his humiliation, ended up on the dole. In 1931 Walter Greenwood was elected a Labour councillor for St Matthias ward to Salford City Council. In fact, he wrote most of *Love on the Dole* at Ashfield Labour Club. He had determined to escape from the '*jungles of tiny houses cramped and huddled together*', in which '*men and women are born, live, love and die and pay preposterous rents for the privilege of calling the grimy houses "home".*' (Chapter 1 *Love on the Dole*).

Encouraged in his love of books and writing by his family, Greenwood wrote a number of novels, but the one for which he is best remembered is *Love on the Dole*, written in 1933 at the height of the depression, which was set in Salford and featured Hanky Park, which took its name from the adjoining Hankinson Street. Hankinson Street is now lost under W.H.Smith and Marks and Spencer in the Salford shopping precinct, while Ellor Street is a car park. Greenwood painted a somewhat gloomy picture of the city. However, like Lowry, he also painted a picture of corner shops, cobbled streets and donkey-stoned doorsteps; a world where life could be hard and without many trappings, but where there was a real sense of community, camaraderie and friendship. It is a world that has now disappeared to be replaced with high-rise blocks of flats, social exclusion, rival gangs and gun law.

Joule, James Prescott (1818–1889)

James Joule was born in 1818 in New Bailey Street in Salford, the son of a local brewer. John Dalton taught him mathematics and algebra, and he won a prize for his first experiments in electro-magnetism. He developed a keen interest in science, and by 1840 he had a laboratory at Pendlebury where he studied units of force and their effect on heat and formulated the theory of heat dynamics - that heat is produced when force is applied. He defined the unit of energy now named after him as the 'joule' or 'J'. For this work, he was awarded the Royal Medal of the Royal Society in

A plaque on the home of J.P. Joule, 1958. (Manchester Archives and Local Studies Library, Central Library)

JAMES PRESCOTT JOULE
SCIENTIST
BORN IN SALFORD IN 1818
DIED IN 1889
LIVED AND WORKED IN THIS HOUSE

1852, and in 1860 he was elected President of the Literary and Philosophical Society. Joule was made President of the British Association in 1872. He was also a keen painter and photographer.

Lowry, L.S. (1887–1976)

Lawrence Stephen Lowry was the only child of Irish parents and was born in Rusholme. He was educated at a school in Victoria Park and then attended Manchester College of Art and Salford School of Art. He worked as a rent collector from 1915–1920 before he began to paint full time. Lowry moved to Salford in 1909 and lived in Pendlebury in the City of Salford for 40 years, becoming renowned for his paintings of the Salford and Manchester millscapes. In 1945 he was awarded an honorary MA by Manchester University and he became a member of the Royal Academy in 1962. He finally settled in Mottram on the edge of the wild and beautiful Longdendale Valley linking Manchester to West Yorkshire. Here he continued to paint millscapes, which he could not see (the mills had disappeared from the Valley by this time) but he could still feel. He died in 1976 and a Blue Plaque marks the house where he spent his final years.

MacColl, Ewan (*c.*1915–1989)

Born Jimmie Miller to Scottish parents in Salford, Ewan MacColl spent a lot of time as a young adult reading in Manchester Public Libraries. He found it difficult to get work during the depression and did a lot of odd-jobbing while he became heavily involved in political and theatrical activities. Miller formed his own street theatre group called the Red Megaphones and began writing satirical songs and political features for factory newspapers. In 1932–3 he took part in demonstrations by the unemployed and the hunger marches like those of Jarrow; and in 1934 he met Joan Littlewood, an ex-RADA actress. They married and set up the worker's experimental Theatre of Action. Miller was by now writing theatrical sketches and dramatic poems. In 1935 they moved to London briefly, but on their return in 1936 the couple set up Theatre Union, a 'theatre of the people', in Salford and Miller started writing plays, such as *Last Edition* and *Uranium 235,* which they both acted in and directed.

In 1939 *Last Edition* (which focused on the political events leading up to the pre-war Munich Agreement) was stopped by the police. Miller and his wife were accused of a breach of the peace, fined and banned from theatrical activities for two years. The outbreak of World War Two disbanded the theatre group, but they all kept in touch and in 1945 they got together again, polled their army gratuities and set up Theatre Workshop. Its aim was to reflect the rapid changes of the 20th century though dramatic techniques with a focus on traditional and natural rhythms of speech. Around this time Miller changed his name to Ewan MacColl.

During the late 1940s MacColl and Joan Littlewood divorced. He was to marry twice more: to dancer Jean Newlove in 1949, with whom he had two children who both became musicians, and, in the late 1950s, to North American folk singer Peggy Seeger, with whom he had three children. In 1953 MacColl switched from theatre to the blues and folk revival that was taking place and founded the Ballads and Blues Club, where he sang regularly until his death in 1989. He and Peggy became a well-known singing duo, gave concerts, led workshops and wrote Radio Ballads, dubbed 'folk documentaries', for the BBC. Ewan MacColl continued his interest in theatre and wrote his last play, *The Shipmaster,* in 1980; but it is for his songs, such as *The First Time Ever I Saw Your Face*, *Manchester Rambler* and the famous *Dirty Old Town* (about Salford) that he is probably best remembered.

Raffald, Elizabeth (1733–1781)

Born in Doncaster, Elizabeth Raffald trained as a housekeeper. She met and married gardener John Raffald at Arley House in Cheshire. They had six children and moved to Salford in 1763. Their house stood behind the workhouse off Green Lane. There she wrote and published *The Experienced English Housekeeper* and a book on midwifery and she also compiled a *Directory of Manchester* and the first *Registry for Servants*.

Robert Powell (1944–)

The well-known actor Robert Powell was born on 1 June 1944. He lived at 15 Cholmondley Road and later at 34 Lullington Road in Salford, attending Lancaster Road School, then Manchester Grammar School and finally Manchester University. As a child he played in Buile Hill Park. He is a keen fan of Salford Rugby Club. Some of Robert Powell's best-known films include: *The Italian Job* (1969), *Jesus of Nazareth* (1977) and *The Thirty Nine Steps* (1978).

Albert Finney (1936–)

He was born in Salford and lived in Romney Street, Charlestown, and Gore Crescent, Weaste, attending Tootle Drive Primary School, Salford Grammar School and later RADA. During the 1980s he was a member of the Royal Shakespeare Company. Albert Finney is well-known for a host of films and plays including *Saturday Night and Sunday Morning* (1960); *Tom Jones* (1963); *Luther* (1964) and *A Day in the death of Joe Egg* (1968). The actor also gave a memorable performance as Hercule Poirot in Agatha Christie's *Murder on the Orient Express*.

Christopher Eccleston (1964–)

The 2005 *Dr Who* was born at 59 Blodwell Street in Salford and later lived at Coniston Avenue in Little Hulton. He attended Joseph Easton High School and trained at the Central School of Speech and Drama. Christopher Eccleston feels that Salford contains '...decency, honesty and close family...'.

Peter Maxwell Davies (1934–)

The composer and conductor grew up at Trafford Road and Wyeville Drive in Swinton, attending Moorside Primary School and Leigh Grammar School. His orchestral works include: *Chat Moss*, *Cross Lane Fair*, *Swinton Jig* and *Lowry*.

More briefly the following should also be mentioned:

Claire Huddert, swimmer, who attended Walkden High School in Worsley.

Graham Nash (who lived in Skinner Street) and **Allen Clarke** (who lived in Hulton Street) were both members of the 1960s pop group The Hollies and both attended Ordsall Lane Junior School.

Baroness Brenda Dean, TUC General Secretary and life peer, attended St Andrew's Church of England Primary School in Eccles.

Ayub Khan Din, playwright and actor, attended Ordsall Council School and Ordsall Secondary School.

Mike Leigh OBE, dramatist, theatre and film director, was the son of a Salford doctor. He lived at 10 Park Lane, Broughton, and 398 Great Cheetham Street and he attended North Grecian Street Primary School.

Andrew Hayhurst, cricketer, attended St Mark's Church of England Primary School in Worsley.

Ryan Giggs, footballer, moved to Swinton when he was seven and attended Grosvenor Road Primary School. He played for Salford School-boys as a youngster.

Hazel Blears MP was born at 27 Hancock Street, Brindleheath, in Pendleton. She attended St Anne's Church of England Primary School, Brindle Heath; Cromwell Road Junior School in Swinton; Wardley Grammar School and Eccles VI Form College.

Frank Fielder, broadcaster, attended St Thomas of Canterbury School.

Ann Ratner, hair salon owner (The Hair Cuttery), lived in Gordon Street, Lower Broughton, and attended St Clement's Primary School.

Rasshied Ali Dinn, designer, was born in Salford and lived over a fish and chip shop in Monmouth Street, Ordsall, attending St Cyprian Church of England Primary School and Ordsall Secondary School.

Simon Hatherstone, journalist, lived in Old Hall Road, Salford, and attended Kersal High School.

Nathan McEvoy, rugby player, was a Salford born and bred lad, who attended All Souls Primary School, Weaste, and Our Lady of Mount Carmel High School.

David White, footballer, was born in Urmston and brought up opposite the Bridgewater Canal on Barton Road. He attended Godfrey Ermen Church of England Primary School.

Salford Stories

Salford seems to be singularly lacking in stories and legends and this maybe because the small village had only an oral tradition, which was swamped by the inrush of the Industrial Revolution. One of the best known Salford tales must be the legend of Guy Fawkes and this is told separately in the section on Ordsall Hall.

The Victoria Theatre Ghost

The Victoria Theatre in Salford (which closed in 1972) was haunted by the ghost of a 'friendly white lady'. She was named Phyllis and was believed to be the ghost of an Edwardian programme seller. Phyllis developed a crush on a well-known leading Edwardian actor, who took brief advantage of this and then rejected her. She was heartbroken and committed suicide by throwing herself from the upper balcony. 'Phyllis' has been seen on numerous occasions in the theatre, usually in the bar, an appropriate enough place for spirits. Her appearance was usually prefaced by the smell of her perfume, described by one stage manager as 'strange and seductive'.

The Victoria Theatre opened on 2 September 1895 and could seat 1,700 people. In 1904 the famous Houdini appeared there and staged an amazing escape from a locked coffin on the stage. As the moving pictures gained in popularity, the Victoria became two cinemas but returned to being a 'live theatre' after one of the cinemas was destroyed in a spectacular fire in 1941. Joseph Locke, Frank Randle and Robb Wilton, all top stars of their day, played there.

Murder at the Jolly Carter

The Jolly Carter was a public house kept by Joseph Blears at Winton, now part of Worsley. In 1826 it was the setting for a brutal murder and robbery. The inn was popular with drivers of carts carrying coals from the Worsley coal mines to Stretford and Manchester – hence its name. Packmen also stayed there. They were travelling merchants who collected woven cloth from farms and cottages to take to market in the towns and cities. Two such packmen, brothers Alexander and Michael M'Keand, often stayed at the Jolly Carter. On the night of 22 May 1826 they sat drinking late in the bar. The landlord was already asleep in bed having had a tiring day with good takings. His wife was tidying the bar parlour before closing for the night. The two members of staff, a maidservant named Elizabeth Bates and a boy called William Higgins, were also in bed.

Suddenly, Michael got up and went to the bar where, intending to rob the takings, he attacked Mrs Blears, stabbing her in the head with a knife. Alexander went upstairs to the servants' bedroom and cut the serving girl's throat. Her screaming and struggling awoke William who, seeing what was happening, rushed from the bedroom, leaped over the staircase and ran from the house with Alexander in hot pursuit. Alarmed, Michael left Mrs Blears, with the knife still sticking in her head, and joined his bother in chasing the boy. Higgins hid himself well in a dry ditch and the murderous pair failed to find him. Convinced that he had escaped and raised the alarm, they made off in haste.

Mrs Blears was badly wounded but still alive, and she survived the attack. Elizabeth Bates, the maidservant, wasn't so fortunate, she was already dead. The savagery of the attack on two defenceless women aroused great anger and horror. A week later a man from the village of Kitling, near the moors of Kirkby Stephen in Westmorland, saw two men bathing their feet in a stream and recognised them as the M'Keand brothers from a description issued by the police. Alexander and Michael M'Keand were finally arrested after a monumental struggle. In August 1827 they were tried and executed at Lancaster on 21 August. Afterwards, Alexander M'Keand's body was sent to Manchester infirmary for dissection. A popular song about the murders included the following lines:

'Oh Betsy Bates we murdered thee,
For which we're on the fatal tree

We stabbed the mistress in the bar,
And gave her nay a cruel scar;
And in her head we left the knife,
But William Higgins saved her life....'

Treading the Boards
John Fisher was born the son of a Salford trader, who had ambitions for his son to become a rope maker. John wasn't interested. He wanted a life of excitement treading the boards. He left his home and spent some time appearing in both the circus and the theatre, deciding, finally, to become an actor after playing Joey in the play *Giles and Joey*. However, John wasn't cut out for the 'big time' After years of 'rambling, toil and sorrow,' he returned, disillusioned, to Manchester and eventually managed to get a job as a 'utility and prompter' under Barney Egan. It was the wrong side of the spotlight and he began to realise that he was just another 'wannabe'. He gritted his teeth and tried to stick it out, but then he

suddenly disappeared. A few days later he was found drowned in the River Irwell near the suspension bridge not far from where he was born. John Fisher had become another sad statistic of thwarted ambition.

Index